CONSTRUCTING CO-CULTURAL THEORY

CONSTRUCTING CO-CULTURAL THEORY

An Explication of Culture, Power, and Communication

MARK P. ORBE

SAGE Publications
International Educational and Professional Publisher
Thousand Oaks London New Delhi

For information, address to:

SAGE Publications, Inc.
2455 Teller Road
Thousand Oaks, California 91320
E-mail: order@sagepub.com

SAGE Publications Ltd.
6 Bonhill Street
London EC2A 4PU
United Kingdom

SAGE Publications India Pvt. Ltd.
M-32 Market
Greater Kailash I
New Delhi 110 048 India

Printed in the United States of America

Library of Congress Cataloging-in-Publication Data

Orbe, Mark P.
Constructing co-cultural theory: An explication of culture, power, and communication / by Mark P. Orbe.
p. cm.
Includes bibliographical references and index.
ISBN 0-7619-1067-0 (cloth: alk. paper). — ISBN 0-7619-1068-9 (pbk.: alk. paper)
1. Communication and culture. 2. Intercultural communication. 3. Ethnicity. 4. Multiculturalism. 5. Stereotype (Psychology) 6. Interpersonal communication. 7. Sexism in communication. I. Title.
HM258.O63 1997
302.2—dc21 97-21128

98 99 00 01 02 03 04 10 9 8 7 6 5 4 3 2 1

Acquiring Editor: Margaret Seawell
Editorial Assistant: Renée Piernot
Production Editor: Sanford Robinson
Production Assistant: Lynn Miyata
Typesetter/Designer: Marion Warren
Cover Designer: Candice Harman
Print Buyer: Anna Chin

Contents

Chapter 1

An Introduction to Co-cultural Communication

Culture and communication are inextricably linked (Brislin, 1993). The ability to comprehend one concept is contingent on understanding its relationship to the other. Within the United States several domestic co-cultures exist on the basis of age, class, ethnicity, religion, abilities, affection or sexual orientation, and other unifying elements (Johnson, 1989; Orbe, 1994a). In the past, researchers have used a variety of terms to describe co-cultural communication: *intracultural* (Sitaram & Cogdell, 1976); *subordinate, inferior, minority* (Stanback & Pearce, 1981); *subcultural* (Pearson & Nelson, 1991); *nondominant* (Folb, 1994); and *muted group* (Kramarae, 1981). The word *co-culture* is used here to avoid the negative or inferior connotations of past descriptions (e.g., *sub*culture, *minor*ity) while also acknowledging the great diversity of influential cultures that simultaneously exist in this country. Although these co-cultures exist all around us, their experiences are often made invisible by the pervasiveness of the dominant culture (Samovar & Porter, 1994).

The use of the word *co-cultures* is especially significant given the breadth of the theoretical framework presented in this book. Co-cultural communication theory is based on the belief that the United States is a country of many cultures, each of which exists simultaneously within and apart from other cultures. The word *co-culture* is embraced over other terminologies to signify the notion that no one culture in our society is inherently superior to other coexisting cultures. Co-cultures are not less important in the ways in which they affect group members' communication, as connoted by the terms *subculture* and *minority communication.* Because an assortment of co-cultures simultaneously exists in our society, co-cultural communication theory also is grounded in the notion that over time one co-culture (that of European-American heterosexual middle- or upper-class males) has acquired dominant group status in the major societal institutions (i.e., political, corporate, religious, and legal institutions) across the land. This central position of one dominant co-cultural group has rendered other co-cultural groups as marginalized with the predominant societal structures; this does not mean, however, that other co-cultural groups' functioning in other venues are less than effective. Co-cultural communication, in its most generic form, refers to interactions among persons from different co-cultures. The focus of the theoretical framework presented in this book, however, is on describing one specific form of co-cultural communication: the communication between dominant group and co-cultural group members *from the perspective of co-cultural group members.* (Chapter 4 explicates the notion of co-cultural communication in greater detail.)

Communication scholars have given significant attention to the communication strategies that different groups use during what has become regarded as intercultural interactions (Collier, Ribeau, & Hecht, 1986; Gudykunst & Hammer, 1987; Hecht, Collier, & Ribeau, 1993; Samovar & Porter, 1994). Other researchers, as illustrated by the works of Arendt (1986), de Certeau (1984), and Foucault (1979), have focused on how those without power communicate. Borisoff and Merrill (1992) suggest that differences between co-cultural and dominant group members' communication are essentially differences in relative power between these two groups in a given situational context. As different underrepresented group members continue to enter new areas of association (and in greater numbers) with clear opposition to expectations for assimilation, research efforts that continue to explore the ways in which different persons communicate will become even more important in understanding the intricacies of ingroup or outgroup relations (Orbe, 1995).

Most of the existing research efforts exploring culture's impact on communication processes have been criticized for focusing primarily on the dominant perspective (James, 1994; Orbe, 1995; Skinner, 1982). In this regard traditional research has treated the communication of dominant group members as intricately complex and diversified, while formulating a generalized universal iconography (Orbe, 1995) of the communication of co-cultural groups. From the perspective of underrepresented group members, these representations typically suffer from a strong ethnocentric bias (James, 1994). In addition, what so often gets lost in the traditional research on culture and communication is the "interplay of power relations" (Moon, 1996, p. 75), a reality that is oftentimes made invisible by white male heterosexual privilege (McIntosh, 1988). Some recent efforts, however, approach the topic from alternate (co-cultural group) perspectives (e.g., Gonzalez, Houston, & Chen, 1994; Ringer, 1994) with an inherent focus on exposing how societal power influences everyday communication. Such a variety of approaches is crucial when attempting to gain insight into the "deep structures" (Pennington, 1979, p. 392) that inform intercultural communication. In fact, Frankenberg (1993) attests that "the oppressed can see with the greatest clarity, not only their own position but . . . indeed the shape of social systems as a whole" (p. 8). Clearly, research that focuses on "nondominant" group communicative experiences seeks to inform the development of communication theory, explore the dynamics of power, culture, and communication, and celebrate the spirit of human ingenuity (Stanback & Pearce, 1981).

Some significant research exists from a dominant and co-cultural group perspective on the communication processes of different *singular* co-cultural groups. This research provides great insight into how different cultural groups within our society communicate both internally (ingroup) and externally (outgroup). For instance, some attention has been paid to the communicative experiences of women (Arliss & Borisoff, 1993; Gilligan, 1982; Kramarae, 1981), people of color (Gong, 1994; Hecht et al., 1993; Hecht, Ribeau, & Sedano, 1990; Houston, 1994; Kochman, 1990; Nakayama, 1994), persons with disabilities (Braithwaite, 1990, 1991; Jankowski, 1991), working-class communities (Lovdal, 1989; Philipsen, 1975), gays, lesbians, and bisexuals (Chesebro, 1981; Ringer, 1994; Spradlin, 1995; Woods, 1993), retired persons (Ayers, 1994; Hummert, Wiemann, & Nussbaum, 1994), and young people (Baxter & Goldsmith, 1990). The unique contribution of the ongoing research reported in this book (Ford-Ahmed & Orbe, 1992; Orbe, 1994b, in press; Roberts & Orbe, 1996) is that it explores the common patterns of communication *across* these different marginalized groups, something currently not extensively undertaken in the field of communication. Specifically, co-cultural theory works to create a framework that promotes a greater understanding of the intricate processes by which co-cultural group members (women, people of color, gays, lesbians, bisexuals, etc.) negotiate attempts by others to render their voices muted within dominant societal structures. Inherent in its analysis of co-cultural communication is attention to the commonalities and differences between and among co-cultural groups.

Constructing Co-cultural Theory is designed to present a theoretical framework that describes how those without societal power communicate with persons who are privileged within dominant structures. The layout of the book is organized in a way that informs the reader about the developmental process of co-cultural theory. In this regard, the co-cultural communication theoretical framework is displayed within a specific contextual position. This chapter includes some fundamental concepts related to co-cultural communication and an abbreviated overview of the theory. Descriptions of *A Tale of "O": On Being Different* a short video on diversity that lends insight into the everyday dynamics of majority or minority relations, function as a point of introduction to this analysis.

A Tale of "O": On Being Different

A Tale of "O": On Being Different (Fant, Cohen, Cox, & Kanter, 1979) is a widely used diversity training tool produced by Goodmeasure, Inc., and provides a valuable point of initiation into an examination of co-cultural communication. Recounting a "familiar drama, performed every day in every place," this short video explains ingroup or outgroup relations between those in the majority (Xs) and those in the minority (Os). According to its producers, *A Tale of "O": On Being Different* describes the relational dynamics of difference on the basis of majority or minority status and is directly applicable to differences on the basis of cultural diversity (race, sex, age, etc.). Due to its insightful descriptions of dominant group or co-cultural group communicative relations, some highlights of the video are shared here as a starting point for the explication of co-cultural theory.

Intrinsic to their minority status (on the basis of sheer numbers), *O*s stand out more when functioning in dominant structures largely maintained by *X*s. In a setting that displays remnants of *X*s' lived experiences as the norm, *O*'s uniqueness gets it eXtra attention." Nevertheless, it is important to recognize that the increased visibility of *O*s is not positively associated with their abilities; instead, their distinctiveness results in greater public scrutiny. An *O* may sometimes feel as if he or she is experiencing a "fishbowl syndrome" where others are constantly watching every behavior—that is magnified by the fishbowl itself—from all sides. According to Fant et al. (1979), *O*s may experience *O*verload while attempting to negotiate their minority status. Such a position typically includes striving to achieve at *X*'s performance level and attempting to meet *X*'s perceptions of a good *O*. These perceptions usually involve balancing the additional expectations of *O*s, and includes serving as the token *O* on committees, articulating the *O*'s perspective, and assuming the role of mentor for all other *O*s.

The mere presence of *O*s in structures historically populated by *X*s results in a magnified ingroup solidarity. Following the appearance of one or more *O*s, *X*s begin to recognize commonalities with other *X*s that were previously not given consciousness. In addition, *X*s may perceive the *X* culture as challenged by the existence of *O*s. According to the producers of *A Tale of "O": On Being Different* (Fant et al., 1979), "Some of what seems like prejudice against an *O* is really just the *X*s' discomfort of having to think about things that used to be natural." The *X*s often respond to this indirect challenge by exaggerating the mores of their (once invisible) culture while in the presence of *O*s to emphasize their cultural differences. In addition to the constant reminders of their outgroup status, *O*s must somehow also manage the existing stereotypes of *O*s held by many *X*s.

Often an *O* is assumed to be something that she or he is not. Stereotyping is a natural human tendency and is elevated in situations where contact is largely unsubstantial and limited to a few group members. With general applicability across the source of their cultural difference, *O*s are commonly labeled along four stereotypical characteristics. First, Xs see Os as helpers. By assuming the role of "servant, supporter, or caretaker," Os are seen as available to strengthen Xs, but their role is clearly less important than the real business of the group. A second O stereotype is that of sex object. The Os are typically seen by Xs as ones to be flirted with, fought over, or admired for their sexuality. The Xs also stereotype Os with the label of mascot. In this regard, Os operate as entertainers, cheerleaders, comedians, or song-and-dance persons. Their primary role is to enhance Xs' self-concept as they achieve great things; Os' possibilities for achievement are diminished as they "cheer from the sidelines." These three stereotypes, helper, sex object, and mascot, situate an O's existence in a distinct subordinate position. Consequently, Xs typically respond by providing protection for their O counterparts, who are perceived within existing stereotypical limits. Nevertheless, it is important to recognize that, in doing so, this "protection" also shields Os from most opportunities that appear potentially dangerous, threatening, or risky (but are subsequently highly advantageous).

The final X stereotype of Os is that of militant. This label describes Os who do not attempt to blend into an eXistence in which their cultural differences are made invisible. The Xs perceive militant Os as self-sufficient, tough, aggressive, and dangerous—persons who must be kept at a distance. Unlike the first three stereotypical characterizations, Xs do not overwhelm militant Os with constant efforts to abet them. The Xs will not offer assistance to the militant O even when circumstances warrant such behavior. "Sorry you're having trouble, but you didn't want preferential treatment," Xs reason. When militant Os, in the absence of structural support from Xs, are posed to fail they, according to Xs, "get what uppity Os deserve."

Despite the stereotypical characterizations inherent in their outgroup status, Os, who are determined to survive and/or succeed within groups dominated by Xs, devise mechanisms to fulfill their objectives. Whereas they readily acknowledge the importance of "the old X-network in getting ahead," some of their strategies involve associations with dominant X group members. *A Tale of "O": On Being Different* relates three "choices open to Os who want to survive." First, Os may focus their efforts toward Overachievement. Recognizing that they must seemingly work twice as hard to get half as far, Os concentrate on "doing more better and faster than any X." Furthermore, Os are forced to compete with other minority group members for the few positions accessible to Os (that are grossly limited compared to those available to Xs). Despite this noteworthy attempt to become an "eXceptional O," this type of charge is unfair within dominant structures that typically reward Xs who are average.

A second "choice" for Os is to converge their efforts toward the goal of assimilation into dominant structures. This alternative involves Os who attempt to act, talk, and dress like Xs. In some instances, Os may isolate themselves from other Os in attempts to set themselves apart from Ordinary Os. In fact, Os may even solidify this differentiation by leading critiques of Os and participating in Offensive jokes Xs tell about Os. Nevertheless, this strategy for survival is oftentimes questioned by Xs who wonder why Os are never content with just being themselves. Other Xs view this behavior as evidence of the existing problems of Os; they reason that "even Os see the problems of being an O."

The final "choice" for Os, according to Fant et al. (1979), is "hiding behind an X" or "dropping out." With this choice an O makes a conscious effort to avoid the instances that are likely to draw increased attention and assumes the role of assisting others to succeed. The decision to avoid competing for the spotlight diminishes the chances of stress, burnout, or the possibility of being overexposed. Choosing between the strategies for survival is not an easy decision for Os. Instead, many feel torn between the expectations of Xs that are important for success and their allegiance to Os.

A Tale of "O": On Being Different is an excellent source for insight into the lived experiences of those traditionally marginalized within and outside of the dominant structures in society. The purpose of the short video is to promote understanding of others' behaviors in environments where a majority or minority situation exists. Although the focus of the information is on "numbers only," the video does lend insight into how dynamics of power are enacted in a majority or minority hierarchy. In fact, the concluding comments of *A Tale of "O": On Being Different* make reference to this element of ingroup or outgroup relations: "Understanding why numbers make a difference is a good start to help all of us . . . [however] numbers alone are not the whole story" (Fant et al., 1979).

According to the producers of the film, examinations of the politics of difference must also address the following questions: How is opportunity distributed? What career and educational pathways are made accessible? Who have the jobs with power in the group? How do the structures of resources and support influence who achieves what in groups? Although these questions are not easily answered, co-cultural theory offers a theoretical framework that encourages an understanding of them and how *Os* use specific communicative practices to confront the current politics of difference. As illustrated through the animated vignettes included in *A Tale of "O": On Being Different,* preliminary—albeit somewhat sketchy—work exists on co-cultural communication. Co-cultural theory uses this preliminary work as a building block in its attempt to devise a framework that describes the phenomenon from the standpoint of co-cultural group members.

Overview of Co-cultural Theory

Co-cultural theory represents an eclectic approach to communication theory in that it draws from various existing conceptual frameworks related to culture, power, and communication. Nevertheless, the work described in this text is most closely aligned with the perspective taken by critical or cultural interpretative researchers. Specifically, co-cultural theory is grounded in the work of feminist scholars, namely, muted-group theory (Kramarae, 1981) and standpoint theory (Smith, 1987). To understand the underpinning of a co-cultural theoretical framework, some knowledge of these recent movements is necessary.

Muted-Group Theory

Muted-group theory was initially established by the anthropologists Shirley and Edwin Ardener and later adopted by communication scholars to address the experiences of women (Kramarae, 1981) and African American men (Orbe, 1994b). Shirley Ardener (1975) and Edwin Ardener (1978) suggest that in every society a social hierarchy exists that privileges some groups over others. Those groups that function at the top of the social hierarchy determine to a great extent the communication system of the entire society. Over time, the structures of this system—that reflect the "worldview" of dominant group members—are reinforced as the appropriate communicative system for both dominant and nondominant group members (E. Ardener, 1978).

This process of creating and reinforcing public communication systems renders those persons outside the dominant group "inarticulate," since they are constrained by the dominant communicative structures that are not representative of their worldview (S. Ardener, 1975). In other words, the voices of marginalized group members are muted or, in the least, distorted within a communication system that excludes their lived experiences as legitimate. In addition to the effects of inarticulation, the language system also encourages dominant group members to establish evaluative criteria for the communication of themselves and others. The result of these oppressive structures is that they directly and/or indirectly "block the power of actualization of the other" (Kramarae, 1981, p. 25).

A muted-group framework exists within any society that includes asymmetrical power relationships. Kramarae's (1981) research on women and Orbe's (1994b) work on African American men use this muted-group framework in their inquiries into the communicative experiences of nondominant or co-cultural group members. In addition to addressing how public communication systems silence the voices of these groups, this line of research also examines how "muted" group members use specific verbal and nonverbal communication strategies to surmount attempts to make them inarticulate. (This research will be covered in greater detail in Chapter 2.) Throughout this book, the term *co-cultural communication* is used interchangeably with *muted-group communication;* however, co-cultural is the preferred terminology since muted-group positioning is not a fixed condition.

The fundamental concepts included in muted-group theory represent an integral element in the formulation of co-cultural theory. In the simplest of terms, co-cultural theory seeks to provide a framework to gain insight into how those with little or no societal power communicate with those aligned with the power of dominant societal structures. Muted-group theory is essential to this examination, as it acknowledges and describes asymmetrical power relations within social hierarchies. An important contribution of co-cultural theory is that it approaches the communication among these groups *from the perspective of those without power.* Feminist standpoint theory represents a conceptual framework that lends itself to such an approach.

Standpoint Theory

Standpoint theory is established in the work of recent research by feminist sociology scholars (Harding, 1987, 1991; Hartsock, 1983;

Smith, 1987). Exploring the daily life experiences of persons situated in subordinate positions (Smith, 1987), standpoint theory focuses on acknowledging a specific societal capacity that serves as a subjective vantage point from which persons interact with themselves and the world. Recognition of the impact of a person's field of experience, according to this perspective, is essential to understanding his or her perceptions of daily communication experiences.

Standpoint theory, as it contributes to co-cultural theory, is guided by several tenets. First, research must begin from a person's concrete lived experiences and include the experiences of marginalized group members in the process of inquiry in meaningful ways. Such positioning recognizes a myriad of standpoints among and within different co-cultural groups. Second, the inclusion of co-cultural group experiences is crucial since those with and without societal power have conflicting worldviews; the vast majority of existing scholarship presents only the dominant perspective. Like Kramarae (1981), standpoint theorists embrace the notion of alternative understandings of the world that are situated in the everyday or everynight activities of co-cultural and dominant group members. A third tenet extends this fundamental concept to describe the significance of including the perspectives of marginalized group members in scholarly inquiry. Standpoint theory contends that the value of these co-cultural perspectives is crucial, since marginalized group members have the ability to see dominant societal structures from the positioning of an "outsider-within" perspective (Collins, 1986). In other words, marginalized group members who gain access (albeit sometimes fleeting) into dominant structures have the unique opportunity to perceive the settings from a near *and* obscure vantage point. Such experiential "cultural knowledge" (Nakayama, 1995, p. 173) about communication is invaluable.

The underlying concepts associated with muted-group and standpoint theory serve as a foundation for co-cultural theory. Grounded in an epistemological stance that seeks to empower those traditionally marginalized on the fringe of dominant societal structures, these theories demonstrate a valuable framework for researching the communicative lived experiences of co-cultural group members. The beginnings of co-cultural communication research can be seen in the preliminary work of various scholars, most notably Stanback and Pearce (1981), as explained in Chapter 2. Extending the work of muted-group and standpoint theory, as well as the limited studies on the communication of marginalized groups, co-cultural theory represents a conceptual development on the basis of several fundamental assumptions.

Premises

The fundamental concepts of co-cultural theory are grounded in five epistemological assumptions. The articulation of these theoretical premises is important as they inform the reader about the distinct consciousness from which a co-cultural communication theoretical framework emerged. Some of the basic assumptions presented here draw from the work of muted-group theory; others materialized as "basic truths" from the standpoint of persons whose societal existence is typically marginalized by dominant public structures. In any case, co-cultural theory is situated within these five premises.

1. In each society, a hierarchy exists that privileges certain groups of people; in the United States these groups include men, European Americans, heterosexuals, the able-bodied, and middle and upper class.
2. On the basis of these varying levels of privilege, dominant group members occupy positions of power that they use—consciously or unconsciously—to create and maintain communication systems that reflect, reinforce, and promote their field of experiences.
3. Directly and/or indirectly, these dominant communication structures impede the progress of those persons whose lived experiences are not reflected in the public communicative systems.
4. Although representing a widely diverse array of lived experiences, co-cultural group members—including women, people of color, gays, lesbians, bisexuals, people with disabilities, and those from a lower socioeconomic status—will share a similar societal position that renders them marginalized and underrepresented within dominant structures.
5. To confront oppressive dominant structures and achieve any measure of "success," co-cultural group members strategically adopt certain communication behaviors when functioning within the confines of public communicative structures.

Inherent in this theoretical position, as embodied in the five premises described, is the substantiation of all possible standpoints within the co-cultural experience. A co-cultural epistemology, consistent with its grounding in feminist standpoint theory, promotes a theoretical foundation that simultaneously unites *and* differentiates marginalized group experiences without essentializing them. In other words, co-cultural theory seeks to uncover the commonalities among co-cultural group members as they function in dominant society while substantiating the vast diversity of experiences between and among groups. In this regard, similarities among the oppressive practices of sexism, racism, heterosexism, "ableism" and classism—at personal, social, organizational, and institutional levels—are recognized while concurrently acknowledging the different ways in which these conventions are manifested in the daily lives of co-cultural group members. In fact, the premises articulated also symbolize a recognition of the multiplicities of experiences within and among co-cultural groups. Just as there is no one form of dominant group communication (e.g., "men's communication," "European American communication," "heterosexual communication," etc.), any one definitive explanation of co-cultural communication ("women's communication," "African or Latino or Asian or Native American communication," "gay communication," etc.) is problematic in that it promotes a universally accepted cultural iconography (Aptheker, 1989; Orbe, 1995) that renders the diverse communicative experiences of these groups invisible. A phenomenological approach augments this movement away from the construction of a generalized co-cultural "Other."

A Phenomenological Approach

The co-cultural theoretical framework described throughout this book is a consequence of a series of recent research projects (Ford-Ahmed & Orbe, 1992; Orbe, 1994b, in press; Roberts & Orbe, 1996) that used a phenomenological approach to studying the communicative experiences of diverse co-cultural group members. The fundamental conceptual stance inherent in a phenomenological methodology, as it unites with muted-group and standpoint theories, appears especially fitting in the exploration of co-cultural communication described here.

Gonzalez et al. (1994) call for research that invites personal experience into inquiries examining culture, power, and communication. The use of personal experiences as evidence (Foss & Foss, 1994;

Le Guin, 1989) encourages scholarship that emphasizes the "experiential rather than the experimental" (Houston, 1989, p. 190). Such research efforts are likely to yield insight not easily obtained through traditional scientific methods (Orbe, 1995). A phenomenological inquiry represents one methodological avenue that centers on ived experiences.

Classified as a human science (Van Manen, 1990), hermeneutic phenomenology is the study of the lifeworld (*lebenswelt*). Phenomenology focuses on the conscious experience of a person as she or he relates to the lived world (Lanigan, 1979). Phenomenologists historically (Husserl, 1962; Merleau-Ponty, 1948/1962) and more recently (Deetz, 1981; Lanigan, 1979, 1988; Nelson, 1989b) have worked to become a medium for the voice of their co-researchers without necessarily manipulating, altering, or reshaping their life experiences (Gluck & Patai, 1991). "Co-researchers" is used here (instead of other terminology, such as "subjects" or "participants") to designate the interactive role that these persons play in shaping research outcomes. Adopted by a number of recent phenomenological inquiries in the communication of different co-cultural groups (Ford-Ahmed, 1992; Nelson, 1989b; Peterson, 1992), this terminology reflects a general change from traditional empirical research in which objective examinations of nonrelational others is valued.

Phenomenological methodology includes a three-step process of discovery: (a) collection of descriptions of lived experiences, (b) reduction of *capta* into essential themes, and (c) hermeneutic interpretation of themes. This reflective process, described in detail in Chapter 3, is situated in several key assumptions (Van Manen, 1990). In short, phenomenology encourages researchers to acknowledge persons as multidimensional and complex beings with particular social, cultural, and historical life circumstances (Van Manen, 1990). Each co-researcher is viewed as the expert on her or his own life (Foss & Foss, 1994). Such an approach is crucial for gaining insight into populations that have been muted within dominant societal structures. Recently, phenomenological inquiries have effectively focused on inductively discovering the communicative experiences of women (Gluck & Patai, 1991), African Americans (Ford-Ahmed, 1992; Peterson, 1992), and adult students (Stanage, 1987). The four independent, albeit evolving, research projects that formed the cornerstone of co-cultural theory (Ford-Ahmed & Orbe, 1992; Orbe, 1994b, in press; Roberts & Orbe, 1996) add to the evidence that phenomenology is an especially relevant methodology when researching the communicative experiences of marginalized group members. In short, it represents a philosophic and human science research method that constitutes an avenue to provide discursive space where those traditionally muted voices can be heard. In this regard, phenomenology serves the challenges of exploring co-cultural communication well. Through the abovementioned series of phenomenological inquiries, a framework of co-cultural communication was conceptualized.

Selecting Co-cultural Communicative Practices

Co-cultural theory explores the process by which co-cultural group members select certain communicative practices when interacting within the structures of dominant society. To draw from recent research by Deetz (1992), this line of inquiry seeks to explore how different marginalized groups manage "discursive closure" (p. 187). de Certeau (1984) uses the word *tactics* to describe nondominant communication behaviors; he reserves the use of "strategies" to refer to the practices of those with power. Nevertheless, the following excerpt (de Certeau, 1984) indicates that, to a certain extent, "power" can be enacted on a variety of levels (personal, social, institutional).

> Innumerable ways of playing and foiling the other's game . . . characterize the subtle, stubborn, resistant activity of groups [that], since they lack their own space, have to get along in a network of already established forces and representations. *People have to make do with what they have.* [italics added] (p. 11)

A starting point for the emergence of a co-cultural theoretical framework was the identification, via a discovery-oriented phenomenological method, of a myriad of communicative practices that marginalized group members engage in while functioning within dominant societal structures. Through several research efforts, more than 25 different co-cultural communicative practices were distinguished (see Table 1.1). The purpose for explicating these practices is not necessarily to advance a definitive collection of mutually exclusive communicative "performances." The design, instead, is to present specific communicative behaviors as described from the standpoint(s) of co-cultural group members. To this end, some practices—given superficial inspection—apparently appear to overlap or conflict with others. Chapter 4 provides detail of each communicative practice as well as specific narratives from co-cultural group members illustrating each communicative tactic.

Nonetheless, a more thorough analysis of these co-cultural communicative practices reveals that each tactic represents an intricate selection process based on six primary factors. Interdependently connected, the six factors inherent in the process by which co-cultural group members select specific communicative practices are (a) preferred outcome, (b) field of experience, (c) abilities, (d) situational context, (e) perceived costs and rewards, and (f) communication approach. The focus of Chapter 5 is an explication of these six factors and their interdependence in formulating decisions involving a cyclical process of awareness-contemplation-implementation-evaluation. After a deeper analysis of several of these factors (preferred outcome, communication approach, and perceived costs and rewards), a theoretical conceptualization of co-cultural communication orientations emerged. Drawing from the insights of oral narratives provided by a diverse collection of co-cultural group members, nine primary co-cultural communication orientations were conceived: nonassertive assimilation, assertive assimilation, aggressive assimilation, nonassertive accommodation, assertive accommodation, aggressive accommodation, nonassertive separation, assertive separation, and aggressive separation. These co-cultural communication orientations will be described in detail in the latter part of Chapter 5.

The focus of these communication orientations, and how they interact with the remaining influential factors associated with the process of selecting specific communicative practices, represent the core of co-cultural theory. The levels of saliency for each factor may vary greatly among and within different co-cultural group members depending on the specific field of experience and situational circumstances. In any case, the conceptual framework that emerges from these abstractions provides an insightful vantage point into co-cultural communication from the standpoint of those typically marginalized within dominant societal structures. In short, the six factors collectively assist in the explication of a pervasive co-cultural communication process:

> Situated within a particular *field of experience* that governs their *perceptions of the costs and rewards* associated with, as well as their *ability* to perform, various communicative practices, co-cultural group members will adopt various communication orientations—on the basis of

(*text continued on p. 18*)

TABLE 1.1 Co-cultural Communicative Practices Summary

Practice	*Brief Description*
Emphasizing commonalities	Focusing on human similarities while downplaying or ignoring co-cultural differences
Developing positive face	Assuming a gracious communicator stance in which one is more considerate, polite, and attentive to dominant group members
Censoring self	Remaining silent when comments from dominant group members are inappropriate, indirectly insulting, or highly offensive
Averting controversy	Averting communication away from controversial or potentially dangerous subject areas
Extensive preparation	Engaging in an extensive amount of detailed (mental or concrete) groundwork prior to interactions with dominant group members
Overcompensating	Conscious attempts—consistently employed in response to a pervasive fear of discrimination—to become a "superstar"
Manipulating stereotypes	Conforming to commonly accepted beliefs about group members as a strategic means to exploit them for personal gain
Bargaining	Striking a covert or overt arrangement with dominant group members in which both parties agree to ignore co-cultural differences
Dissociating	Making a concerted effort to elude any connection with behaviors typically associated with one's co-cultural group
Mirroring	Adopting dominant group codes in attempts to make one's co-cultural identity less (or totally not) visible
Strategic distancing	Avoiding any association with other co-cultural group members in attempts to be perceived as a distinct individual
Ridiculing self	Invoking or participating in discourse, either passively or actively, which is demeaning to co-cultural group members
Increasing visibility	Covertly, yet strategically, maintaining a co-cultural presence within dominant structures

TABLE 1.1 Continued

Practice	*Brief Description*
Dispelling stereotypes	Myths of generalized group characteristics and behaviors are countered through the process of just being oneself
Communicating self	Interacting with dominant group members in an authentic, open, and genuine manner; used by those with strong self-concepts
Intragroup networking	Identifying and working with other co-cultural group members who share common philosophies, convictions, and goals
Using liaisons	Identifying specific dominant group members who can be trusted for support, guidance, and assistance
Educating others	Taking the role of teacher in co-cultural interactions; enlightening dominant group members of co-cultural norms, values, and so forth
Confronting	Using the necessary aggressive methods, including ones that seemingly violate the "rights" of others, to assert one's voice
Gaining advantage	Inserting references to co-cultural oppression to provoke dominant group reactions and gain advantage
Avoiding	Maintaining a distance from dominant group members; refraining from activities and/or locations where interaction is likely
Maintaining barriers	Imposing, through the use of verbal and nonverbal cues, a psychological distance from dominant group members
Exemplifying strengths	Promoting the recognition of co-cultural group strengths, past accomplishments, and contributions to society
Embracing stereotypes	Applying a negotiated reading to dominant group perceptions and merging them into a positive co-cultural self-concept
Attacking	Inflicting psychological pain through personal attacks on dominant group members' self-concept
Sabotaging others	Undermining the ability of dominant group members to take full advantage of their privilege inherent in dominant structures

their *preferred outcomes* and *communication approaches*—to fit the circumstances of a specific *situation.*

Such an explication of co-cultural communication serves the objectives of this line of scholarly inquiry. First, it represents a theoretical conceptualization of the communication practices ecumenical enough to apply to the various marginalized groups described earlier. Second, and just as important, the framework signifies the legitimacy of all co-cultural standpoints regardless of outgroup *or* ingroup perceptions to the contrary. In this regard, the nucleus of co-cultural theory hinges on the conviction that there is no one "ideal" form of co-cultural communication. This belief is apparent in the descriptions of the practices in Chapter 4, as well as the influential factors explicated in Chapter 5. "Effective" and/or "appropriate" communication is not defined within the structures of the co-cultural theory. Instead, a framework is presented that allows such discernment to be made from the particular standpoint(s) of co-cultural group members themselves.

Chapter 1 was designed to present the reader with an introduction to, or abbreviated review of, the concept of co-cultural communication. In addition, a descriptive overview of the process that generated a co-cultural theoretical framework was presented. The following chapters provide greater details of this process and subsequently yield a more comprehensive treatment of this phenomenon. Such an analysis, along with a discussion of the limitations, extensions, and future directions of co-cultural theory (Chapter 6), is warranted in order to obtain greater understanding of the fundamental ideas presented in this overview.

Chapter 2

Foundations of Muted-Group and Standpoint Theory

The development of co-cultural theory is grounded in the work of scholars in the fields of anthropology, sociology, and communication. Such an acknowledgment is important in encouraging the reader to identify and understand how the co-cultural theoretical framework described in this book is largely within existing work in critical theory. This chapter describes two specific theoretical frameworks—muted-group theory and feminist standpoint theory—that facilitated the development of a paradigm that addresses the communicative experiences of those persons marginalized within the structures of dominant society. After a brief explication of the fundamental ideas associated with these two conceptual frameworks, existing research on co-cultural communication will be presented and reviewed.

Muted-Group Communication

The study of human communication offers insight into the societal organizations that influence daily interaction. Language, according to Kramarae (1981), is used to construct and reinforce social relationships between groups and reveals what is perceived as important by the persons who encode the symbols (Kramarae, 1978). Nevertheless, language does not serve all of its speakers equally since all individuals have not had the opportunity to contribute to its formulation equally (Kramarae, 1981). Building from this premise, muted-group theory is one theoretical framework that can be used to study communication *dominant* and *nondominant* groups.

Anthropologists Shirley Ardener (1978) and Edwin Ardener (1978) posit that a muted-group framework exists within each society. Groups that function at the top of the social hierarchy largely determine the dominant communication system of the entire society (E. Ardener, 1978). Muted-group theory suggests that a language reflects a worldview. Over time, dominant group members formulate—consciously or unconsciously—a communication system that supports their perceptions of the world and conceptualizes it as *the* appropriate language for the rest of society (S. Ardener, 1975). This process subjects nondominant group members to function with a communication system that is not representative of their lived experiences.

Through this development of language, subordinate groups are made "inarticulate" since the communication structures of the mainstream systems reflect a dominant perception of reality (S. Ardener, 1975). Those experiences unique to co-cultural group members often cannot be effectively described within the constraints of the dominant communication structure. Kramarae (1978) concludes that, besides the effects of inarticulation, the language structure allows dominant group members to establish evaluative criteria for language for themselves and others, which reinforces group solidarity and maintains an oppressive force in the lives of co-cultural group members. The concept of "mutedness" illustrates the consequences for others when dominant communication structures maintain perceptual boundaries on the basis of their own perception of reality; in essence, these structures "block the power of actualization of the other" (Kramarae, 1981, p. 25).

Within any society in which asymmetrical power relationships are maintained, a muted-group framework exists (S. Ardener, 1975, 1978). Groups that function at the top of the social hierarchy largely determine the dominant communication system of the entire society (E. Ardener, 1978). This process forces other persons who are not dominant-group members to function within a communication system that is not necessarily representative of their experiences. In this respect, subordinate groups are made "inarticulate" because the language that they use is derived from the dominant group's perception of reality (S. Ardener, 1975). Those experiences unique to subordinate group members often cannot be effectively expressed within the confinements of the dominant communication system. As articulated by S. Ardener (1975), the muted-group theoretical framework may be used to examine communicative relationships between persons with and without societal power.

Muted-group theorists suggest that the framework can be validly applied to many relationships in this society that involve, for example, European Americans or persons of color, child or adult, or working class or middle class (Kramarae, 1981). In a society that privileges certain cultural perspectives (European American, male, heterosexual, able-bodied, youthful, middle and upper class, and/or Christian; Folb, 1994), muted-group theory can be applied to a variety of nondominant groups contingent on specific intergroup dynamics and situational contexts. In this regard, nondominant groups, or co-cultural groups, refer to those groups of people who have not "traditionally had continued access to or influence upon or within the dominant culture" (Folb, 1994, p. 122). In this country (depending on specific situations), these groups include but are not limited to people of color, women, gays, lesbians, bisexuals, people with disabilities, lower and working class, and the young and elderly. Muted-group theory has not received widespread attention from communication scholars in terms of exploring the communicative experiences of various co-cultural group members. Nevertheless, it has been used as a significant source of foundation to study women's communication (Kramarae, 1981) and more recently African American male communication (Orbe, 1994b). The studies on these two muted or co-cultural groups is important to consider as they reveal the development of ideas leading to co-cultural communication theory.

Women as a Muted Group

Kramarae's (1981) *Women and Men Speaking* offers the most extensive application of muted-group theory in the field of communication. According to Kramarae, the role of women in a male-dominated society is often marginalized into one of second-class citizen. Men largely have the power and influence to create systems that work to their advantage. Concerning language use, Kramarae notes that men historically have possessed greater speaking rights and been largely responsible for establishing and maintaining the criteria used to judge men and women's speech. In this respect, women historically have been "muted" by men.

Kramarae (1981) presents three basic assumptions of muted-group theory as applied to women and men. First, women perceive the world differently than men on the basis of different experiences and activities rooted in the division of labor. Second, because of their political dominance, men's system of perception is dominant, impeding the free expression of women's alternate models. Last, to participate in society women must transform their own models in terms of the perceived male system of expression. Kramarae concludes that women traditionally have been muted by a male-dominated communication system, which considers women's work, interests, values, and speech as marginally important. Building on these assumptions and on the basis of additional research findings, Kramarae presents several hypotheses concerning women's communication.

On the basis of the pervasiveness of dominant structures throughout society, Kramarae (1981) proposes seven hypotheses that originate in muted-group theory. First, women will have greater difficulty than men expressing themselves articulately within public modes of expression. Second, women's sense of humor, as well as what relationships between persons, places, and things they consider incongruous, will differ significantly from men's perceptions. The third hypothesis contends that women are more likely than men to experience a significant amount of dissatisfaction with the dominant public modes of expression. Fourth, women will not be as likely to coin words that become widely recognized and used by both women and men. Fifth, women will have less difficulty than men in understanding what members of the other sex mean. The sixth and seventh hypotheses suggest ways in which women will react to their muted-group status as indicated in the first hypothesis. They state that women are likely to find ways to (a) express themselves, verbally and nonverbally, outside the dominant public modes of communication used by males (sixth hypothesis); and/or (b) refuse to live by the ideals of societal organizations, verbally reject those models, and attempt to change dominant communication structures (seventh hypothesis).

Kramarae's (1981) work on muted-group theory, and subsequent research in this domain (e.g., Houston & Kramarae, 1991), serves as a valuable resource for those scholars interested in exploring the lived communicative experiences of people marginalized by dominant structures in this country. Although Kramarae's (and colleague's) premises and hypotheses articulate a perspective specific to the experiences of women, her ideas appear applicable to other muted groups as well. Recent research by Orbe (1994b) and colleagues (Ford-Ahmed & Orbe, 1992) builds on Kramarae's work and uses it as an infrastructure to explore African American male communicative experiences.

African American Men as a Muted Group

As discussed earlier, muted-group positioning exists on several fronts in each society. Exploration of the communication of African Americans and European Americans in the United States is just one of a myriad of application possibilities. Orbe's (1994b) research on African American male communication draws from and subsequently extends the fundamental concepts of muted-group theory.

Using a phenomenological methodology (explained in Chapter 3), Orbe (1994b) initially sought to inductively explore how African American men communicate with non-African Americans. Nevertheless, the research project, through the flexibility inherent in an open-ended conversational interviewing technique, altered its focus. Instead of focusing on interethnic communication between African American men and non-African Americans, the information gained spoke more generally to the lived communicative experiences of African American men—with an emphasis on the importance of communicating with other African American men and women. The significance of intra-muted-group communication is an important consideration to African American men as seen in their explications of the roles that other African Americans play in their competencies to perform in the dominant modes of public expression.

Several specific postulates were advanced in terms of the experiences of muted-group communication. Although the research dealt specifically with African American men, like Kramarae's (1981) studies with women, the conclusions appear fruitfully applicable to other muted groups. Orbe (1994b) discusses six essential themes: (a) the importance of other African Americans, (b) learning how to communicate with non-African Americans, (c) keeping a safe distance from European Americans, (d) playing the part (snap!) while interacting with European Americans, (e) testing the sincerity of non-African Americans, and (f) an intense social responsibility to help other African Americans—that formulate a cultural positioning apparently clear in the ways in which African American men communicate, within and outside the confines of dominant society. Within these six essential themes, one specific contribution, on reflection, appears relative to advancing muted-group theory: the initial identification of distinctive communication strategies used by muted-group members to confront attempts to render them inarticulate. In this regard, a muted-group status is not viewed as fixed but something that is constantly reinforced, augmented, or challenged (Houghton, 1995). Herring, Johnson, and DiBenedetto (1995) conclude that

> mutedness is not simply a condition assigned . . . through early socialization nor an inevitable consequence . . . as [a] member of a culturally subdominant group but, rather, is actively constructed and enforced through everyday discursive interaction. (p. 92)

Orbe (1994b) suggests that African American men engage in a variety of communication strategies to challenge (or possibly reinforce) their muted-group position. In other words, they have embraced a cultural communication system in order to survive and succeed within the oppressive structures of dominant society. How do African American men manage? They communicate with other African Americans for support, motivation, and reassurance. They also employ various strategically positioned approaches in terms of their interactions with non-African Americans, mostly learned from other African Americans. These strategies are influenced by a number of dialectal struggles: Should African American men maintain co-cultural barriers or try to fit into dominant structures? Should they rely solely on other African Americans or can certain European

Americans be trusted as allies? Should communicative energies focus on efforts to enhance intergroup relations or on a continued intense responsibility to assist other African Americans? Whereas no definitive answers to these questions exist, they do create insight into the intricate process of African American male communication specifically and muted-group communication in general. In short, this research makes an important contribution to muted-group theory: Co-cultural groups muted by the communicative structures of dominant society do not necessarily remain muted; they establish a variety of communication strategies to gain their voices within and outside dominant structures.

Standpoint Theory

A general outcome of traditional research is a propensity toward encouraging generalizations on the basis of "scientific" findings with representative samples of subjects. Nevertheless, the line of scholarly research employed in the development of co-cultural communication theory is grounded in a conscious attempt to avoid such inclinations. Instead, it attempts to promote scholarship that acknowledges the specific case as much as the general tendency (Houston, 1989). In this regard, applying the essential concepts of standpoint theory is critical in promoting research on culture and communication that is sensitive to the diversity within co-cultural groups (Orbe, 1995).

Standpoint theory explores the daily life experiences of persons in subordinate positions (Smith, 1987). Rooted in Marxian analysis of working class conditions (Hartsock, 1983), standpoint theory is grounded in the recent work of Collins (1986, 1989, 1990), Harding (1987, 1991), Hartsock (1983), Nielsen (1990), and Smith (1987). Like muted-group theory, standpoint theory has largely been used as a feminist theoretical framework to explore the lived experiences of women as they participate in and oppose their own subordination (Hartsock, 1983), but standpoint theory applications for other subordinate groups are specifically encouraged in work by Smith (1987), Swigonski (1994), and Wood (1992). According to Wallace and Wolf (1995), "Standpoint focuses on perspectives of women, but also could take the perspectives of African American women, poor white women/men, nonwhite women and men and individuals belonging to minority ethnic and religious groups outside modern Western society" (p. 270).

The advantages of grounding co-cultural theory in a standpoint perspective, as it relates to muted-group theory and phenomenology (see Chapter 3), are clear, numerous, and convincing. Smith (1992) describes standpoint theory not as a "totalizing theory," but as "a method of inquiry, always ongoing . . . relevant to the politics and practices of progressive struggle" (p. 8). In this regard, standpoint theory appears to unite the fundamental ideas of muted-group theory and phenomenology with a distinct focus on exposing the importance of everyday life experiences as they relate to, and help construct, our societal positioning. Promoting empowerment is a common thread among these three theoretical approaches, as denoted by Smith (1987) who promotes theory that is capable of

> exploring and mapping actual organization and relations that are invisible but *active* in the everyday/everynight sites where people take up resistance and struggle, capable of producing a knowledge that extends and expands their and our grasp of how things are put together and hence their and our ability to organize and act effectively. (p. 96)

Fundamental Tenets of Standpoint Theory

Standpoint refers to a specific societal position, the result of one's field of experience, which serves as a subjective vantage point from which persons interact with themselves and the world. A standpoint is not simply a subjective position that is interested in promoting bias but an acknowledgment of the sense of being engaged within a specific field of experience. Collins (1990) contends that the conscious recognition of one's standpoint opens the possibilities for a conceptual stance, one in which all groups are acknowledged as possessing varying amounts of "penalty and privilege" (p. 172) as related to dominant group structures. Several tenets of standpoint theory help to explain its centrality in the conceptualization of co-cultural communication theory.

Standpoint as Starting Point

The first principle of standpoint theory is the conviction that research must begin from one's concrete lived experiences, rather than abstract concepts. Such an inductive, open process of discovery encourages scholarship that avoids the problematics of hypothetical investigations designed to solicit preconceived findings. The effect is to decrease the partialities and distortions in research that expose the dimensions of nature and social life (Swigonski, 1994).

Furthermore, standpoint theory seeks to include the experiences of subordinate, or co-cultural, groups, within the process of research inquiry in meaningful ways. In other words, "co-researchers"—those underrepresented group members whose life experiences are being explored—should be brought into a relationship with researchers at each phase of inquiry. The value of involvement is crucial to producing scholarship that conceptualizes but avoids essentializing persons marginalized by dominant society. Wood (1992) describes the process as

> moving away from the distorting practice of simply including neglected groups in research . . . standpoint theory uses marginalized lives as the *starting point* from which to frame research questions and concepts, develop designs, define what counts as data, and interpret findings. In short, standard processes entailed in doing research are reviewed from the perspectives of those outside of the cultural center. (p. 12)

Embracing the lived experiences of co-cultural group members as essential to scholarly inquiry is central to standpoint theory. Such an epistemological approach makes it possible to ask unconventional questions, discover new ways to view nature and social relations, and come to understand knowledge outside the control of the ruling apparatus. Instead, consciousness is given to understanding from the lives of those persons at the societal margin of dominant structures. A focus on the perspectives of the "other" permits seeming irrationalities or inconsistencies on behalf of co-cultural group members to emerge as clear and logical from the vantage of a particular standpoint (Swigonski, 1994).

Conflicting Understandings of the World

As presented in the premise of Kramarae's (1981) work discussed earlier, muted-group members perceive the world differently from dominant group members on the basis of different experiences and activities rooted in the division of labor. Standpoint theory embraces this notion and realizes its relevance to researching the lived experiences of co-cultural group members. In essence, life experience is discerned as the structural force in one's understanding of life. Those persons with the most and the least societal power will potentially have opposed understandings of the world (Swigonski, 1994).

The life perspectives of persons, both nondominant and dominant group members, develop from their daily—often indiscernible, but nonetheless meaningful—activities. Merleau-Ponty (1964) confirms the relevance of scrutinizing the daily, seemingly insignificant, experiences of others since "true little incidents are not life's debris but signs, emblems, and appeals" (p. 313). The appropriate perspective for research activities is exploration of the occurrences of everyday life. A focus on the everyday life experiences helps to reveal the ways in which the public world structures the private, everyday/everynight lives of persons in ways that are not immediately visible as those lives are lived (Swigonski, 1994). Giving consciousness to these daily practices allows scholars to question the larger "taken-for-granted" assumptions that guide our communicative behaviors. Besides a crucial point of understanding the conflicting life perspectives between dominant and nondominant groups, this focus of inquiry also allows a discernment among the various standpoints within a specific co-cultural positioning.

As briefly alluded to earlier, a particular strength of standpoint theory is the inherent affinity to acknowledge the infinite number of possible standpoints within and among co-cultural groups. In this regard, it recognizes the relational links among the ways in which people resist oppressive systems (e.g., hooks, 1984, 1989) yet opposes an essentialist perspective that attempts to generalize lived experiences with little thought to the variance within and among co-cultural groups. In essence, standpoint theory encourages the explication of unifying commonalities while simultaneously discouraging us from thinking that the conditions of all marginalized persons' lives and/or the ways in which all marginalized persons construe their life experiences are the same (Wood, 1992). Through this multilayered position, scholars can recognize and understand the various standpoints among subordinate groups (e.g., women, people of color, gays, lesbians, and bisexuals) and within specific groups (e.g., African Americans). The value of standpoint epistemology is in the ways that it promotes a recognition of what unites and differentiates co-cultural groups without necessarily essentializing them. This is a crucial component of standpoint theory as it fosters a deeper understanding of the communicative experiences of underrepresented groups.

The Merit of an "Outsider-Within" Perspective

Historically, traditional research has excluded marginalized perspectives in the design and direction of both the social order and the production of knowledge. This exclusion has resulted in literature largely void of the experiences of the other. Since life perspectives emerge from one's daily life experiences, knowledge from the standpoint of marginalized group members cannot be fully grasped by those persons privileged by a dominant group positioning. Knowledge production is a hands-on procedure (Harding, 1991; Rose, 1983); through the struggles of oppressed people, a reality of social order is constructed and maintained. This perspective, largely unobtainable by dominant group members, is of great value in that it fills a void in scholarship that lacks the standpoint of subordinate groups.

The value of co-cultural group perspectives also is apparent in an ability of marginalized group members to see dominant societal structures from the eyes of a "stranger" (Collins, 1986). Frankenberg (1993) confirms this notion: "The oppressed can see with the greatest clarity, not only their own position but . . . indeed the shape of social systems as a whole" (p. 8). To survive and succeed in society, those persons marginalized by dominant structures must be attentive to the perspective of the dominant group and their own. In other words, a "double vision" (Swigonski, 1994, p. 390) is established that advocates an awareness of and sensitivity to both the dominant worldview and their own perspective. Because of the privileged stance, those persons positioned in the center of societal structures do not develop a similar double vision but focus solely on the dominant worldview of society. The result of this, as compared to the standpoint of marginalized group members, is a partial view of reality.

An "outsider-within" position is inherent in the perspective of co-cultural group members who function in dominant society (Collins, 1986). Marginalized group members who gain access (albeit fleeting) into dominant structures have the opportunity to experience patterns of beliefs and/or behaviors from a vantage point near *and* obscure in its examination stance. Such is not so for most dominant group members, whose life experiences inherently reflect the images of societal structures. Collins submits that bringing co-cultural group members, who share an outsider-within status, into the center of analysis assists in the process of revealing standpoints of reality that have been obscured by traditional approaches to research. Only when persons function both within and outside of dominant structures is it possible to see the relationship between the larger society and everyday life experiences of its citizens.

The basic ideas associated with the conceptual frameworks of muted-group and standpoint theories serve as the launching pad for co-cultural communication theory. Grounded in a critical perspective, both theories demonstrate a valuable foundation to research the lived experiences of all people traditionally marginalized on the fringe of dominant societal structures. Extending from these theories, co-cultural communication, as a new concept, seeks to relate the experiences of women to other muted groups while simultaneously giving attention to the ways in which persons among and within the groups differ.

Co-cultural Communication

Co-cultural group communication is a relatively new term used to describe the interactions among the diverse collections of persons who call the United States "home." In the past, researchers have used a variety of terms to describe co-cultural communication: *intracultural* (Sitaram & Cogdell, 1976); *subordinate, inferior, minority* (Stanback & Pearce, 1981); *subcultural* (Pearson & Nelson, 1991); nondominant (Folb, 1994), and *muted group* (Kramarae, 1981). The word *co-cultural* has been embraced recently by communication scholars in a conscious attempt to avoid the problematic nature of existing terms that frame marginalized group members as secondary in importance and submissive to the powers of dominant society.

Researchers, many of whom are in the field of communication, have given significant attention to the communicative behaviors, styles, and patterns of different co-cultural groups. For instance, studies have explored the communication of women (Arliss & Borisoff, 1993; Buzzanell, 1994; Campbell, 1986; Gilligan, 1982; Kramarae, 1981), people of color (Collier et al., 1986; Gong, 1994;

Hecht et al., 1993; Hecht, Ribeau, & Alberts, 1989; Hecht et al., 1990; Houston, 1994; Kochman, 1990; Nakayama, 1994), persons with disabilities (Braithwaite, 1990, 1991; Jankowski, 1991), working-class communities (Lovdal, 1989; Philipsen, 1975), gays, lesbians, bisexuals (Chesebro, 1981; Ringer, 1994; Spradlin, 1995; Woods, 1993), retired persons (Ayers, 1994; Hummert et al., 1994), and young people (Baxter & Goldsmith, 1990). This brief listing of research that relates the issues of communication to culture in the United States is hardly inclusive of all the existing literature in this area; such an inventory is not possible in the confines of this chapter. Instead, it is presented here as a representative sample of research completed in the area of co-cultural communication.

More specific to the central focus of co-cultural theory are a few recent research efforts. Folb (1994), Houston and Kramarae (1991), and Woods (1993) have indicated that different co-cultural group members developed specific communication strategies when interacting with dominant group members. The strategies identified are helpful in understanding the communicative experiences of different co-cultural groups. Although this research has generated insight into the communication of different singular co-cultural groups, it does not profess to pertain in equal fashion to all marginalized groups. Only one research study was identified in the literature that explicitly addresses general communication strategies used by members of "subordinate" social groups (Stanback & Pearce, 1981).

"Subordinate" Communication Strategies

The research by Stanback and Pearce (1981) is significant in that it approaches the study of marginalized groups with a recognition that these persons must somehow operate within the constraints imposed by their self-concepts, intentions, and an awareness of dominant group expectations. As articulated by Stanback and Pearce then, and substantiated as still equally fitting today, research that links the communicative experiences of different marginalized groups is important for three reasons. First, exploring the various ways in which those without societal power devise communication tactics when communicating with those with power is a valuable point of examination for communication researchers. Beyond providing an intersection for scholarly inquiry related to culture, power, and communication, it also represents a celebration of human creativity. Second, an analysis of common strategies used by those marginalized by dominant society informs the development of human communication theory. As explicated earlier, such a perspective provides a standpoint largely missing in existing theoretical frameworks. Finally, the characteristics associated with different strategies clarify the relationships within and among co-cultural group members—*from the standpoint of those whose lived experiences reflect a marginalized positioning in the society.*

Through analyzing how underrepresented group members negotiate the expectations of the dominant culture, four specific strategies were identified and discussed (Stanback & Pearce, 1981). The first strategy is called *tomming.* This strategy, manifested by the behaviors of the main character in Harriet Beecher Stowe's *Uncle Tom's Cabin* (published in 1852), occurs when co-cultural group members accept the ways in which they are perceived by dominant group society and behave according to expectations on the basis of those perceptions. To a large extent, tomming reflects a co-cultural self-concept that has internalized the stereotypical characterizations established through the hegemonic pervasiveness of dominant society.

Passing, as described by Stanback and Pearce (1981), occurs when marginalized group members attempt to behave as if they were actually members of dominant society. Passing includes casting off any indication of co-cultural group membership and projecting those behaviors, mannerisms, or values associated with the dominant group. Both tomming and passing reflect strategies that reinforce the existing hierarchical relationships historically maintained throughout society. While tomming participates in this process by exemplifying and maintaining social hierarchy, passing does so by avoiding them.

The third strategy used by those without societal power is similar in some regards to tomming but different in others. *Shucking* (Stanback & Pearce, 1981) occurs when a person "behaviorally conforms to stereotypes while cognitively rejecting the meanings associated with those behaviors/stereotypes" (p. 25). So whereas the behaviors associated with tomming and shucking are similar, the cognitions associated with each are vastly different. Tomming seems to connote a certain level of stereotype internalization. In contrast, shucking represents a strategy in which persons dislike stereotypical acts, resent the behaviors, but feel that such performance is necessary to accomplish particular goals. In other words, co-cultural group members who "tom" do so in consistent fashion; those who are involved in shucking strategically participate in stereotypical behaviors only when necessary or fruitful.

The final strategy used by marginalized group members is *dissembling* (Stanback & Pearce, 1981, p. 26). Dissembling occurs when persons conform to the behavioral expectations on the basis of dominant society stereotypes but disregard the meanings associated with those behaviors. Instead, co-cultural group members embrace the stereotypical behaviors as their own and create an ingroup meaning, oppositional to dominant group codes. Unlike tomming and passing, shucking and dissembling reflect strategies that people use when their cognitive realizations oppose dominant group perceptions.

The unique contribution of this research is that it explores the common patterns of communication across different marginalized groups. However preliminary in nature, it serves as the conceptual foundation for co-cultural theory and initiates a greater understanding of communication from the standpoint of those typically marginalized in research and theory. Some strategies indicate a particular level of internalized oppression, whereas others promote effective interaction with dominant group members without necessarily internalizing the images that society places on them (Stanback & Pearce, 1981). A dialectic appears to emerge by which some co-cultural group members attempt to create communication strategies that are consistent with their self-image, yet do not disrupt the expectations of dominant society. In other words (Stanback & Pearce, 1981), co-cultural group members "somehow . . . work within the constraints imposed by their own intentions and concepts of self and the 'agreed-upon' script lines about how such communication should go" (pp. 21-22). Still others appear to espouse dominant group stereotypes and behave accordingly. Whereas this research does not describe strategies used by marginalized group members with little or no regard for dominant group expectations (nor does it profess to), it represents a point of genesis for exploring the dynamics of culture, power, and communication from a co-cultural standpoint.

This chapter was designed to describe the epistemological underpinnings of the development of co-cultural communication theory. Muted-group theory, especially the work by Kramarae (1981), and feminist standpoint theory represent a foundation for extending the preliminary work on communication from the perspective of marginalized group members completed by Stanback and Pearce (1981). Specifically, the chapter presented the basic principles associated with both theoretical frameworks and related them to a rigorous exploration of co-cultural communicative experience beyond women's communication. Finally, the initial work on subordinate communication strategies by Stanback and Pearce was reviewed as it creates a point of introduction into a more complex inquiry into co-cultural communication. The next chapter describes the process of phenomenological inquiry and focuses on how this methodological approach productively intertwines with the conceptual positioning of muted-group and standpoint theories. Although an exhaustive familiarization with phenomenology inquiry is not necessary, some detailed information is warranted since it represents an integral part of understanding how co-cultural theory is informed by the lived experiences of co-cultural group members.

Chapter 3

Explicating Phenomenological Inquiry

Hermeneutic phenomenology, classified as a human science (Van Manen, 1990), is the study of the lifeworld (*lebenswelt*), the world as we immediately experience it prereflectively rather than as we conceptualize or theorize about it (Husserl, 1970). This chapter briefly reviews the fundamental concepts of phenomenology and presents a detailed account of the three-step process of a phenomenological inquiry. Specific attention is given to how this crucial method is advantageous for communication research, which strives to capture the standpoint of co-cultural group members. In essence, the chapter represents a response to three basic questions concerning phenomenology and the field of communication: (a) What is it, (b) how is it employed, and (c) why is this approach apropos when studying co-cultural communication? The final section of this chapter describes the process from which the foundation for co-cultural communication theory was extracted.

Phenomenology

Phenomenology is the name of the historical movement inaugurated in Germany by several scholars, including Heidegger, Husserl, and Jaspers, and continued in France by Merleau-Ponty and Sartre (Lanigan, 1979). The phenomenological movement was adopted by a number of American communication scholars (Deetz, 1973, 1981; Ford-Ahmed, 1992; Gregg, 1966; Hyde & Smith, 1979; Lanigan, 1988; Nelson, 1989a, 1986; Warnick, 1979). According to Lanigan (1979), phenomenologists approach research with the perspective taken by Husserl: to return to "rigorous science" (Van Manen, 1990) in which analysis focuses on conscious experience rather than hypothetical constructs.

Phenomenology focuses on the conscious experience of a person relating to the lived world that she or he inhabits (Zeitgeist) (Lanigan, 1979). Van Manen (1990) adds that this relationship must occur as people immediately and prereflectively experience their lifeworld before categorization begins. Phenomenological research is involved in explicating phenomena as they present themselves to consciousness (Van Manen, 1990). Although many terms have been used to describe this field of study (e.g., *human science, hermeneutic, existential, semiotic*), the underlying assumptions of phenomenology remain fairly consistent.

Key Assumptions

Phenomenology is based on several key assumptions (Van Manen, 1990). First, phenomenology rejects the notion of an "objective researcher" and the claims of positivist epistemology (Langellier & Hall, 1989). Lengel (1992) reports that "the phenomenological epoche makes no such claims of objectivity because the assumptions grounding phenomenology assert that the researcher is fully immersed in the lifeworld" (p. 3). Phenomenology as a research method requires researchers to acknowledge the ways in which they are positioned within the discourse that they are seeking to understand (Nelson, 1989b). Since the idea of complete "objectivity" is impossible (Patton, 1983), phenomenologists acknowledge preconceived notions and then put them aside or bracket them (Nelson, 1989a). This process, referred to by some as radical empiricism, permits a fuller and fairer treatment of the phenomenon than traditional empiricism allows (Spiegelberg, 1960/1982), mainly because the approach does not hide under an objective cloak.

Second, phenomenology seeks to gain a deeper understanding of the nature and meaning of our everyday experiences (Merleau-Ponty, 1948/1962, 1964). Phenomenological research encourages a certain attentive awareness to the details and seemingly trivial happenings of our everyday lives (Fiske, 1991). Such refocusing allows scholars to make others aware of the inconsequential and taken-for-granted experiences that consume every aspect of our lives (Van Manen, 1990). By eliciting experiential descriptions of everyday life, phenomenologists (e.g., Fiske, 1991) can begin to understand cultural practices and how they operate in the larger context. Van Manen (1990) suggests that the problem of phenomenological inquiry is not always that we know too little about the phenomenon we wish to research but that we know too much. An abundance of knowledge, however, does not necessarily yield understanding. It is often after much refocusing and rebracketing of concepts that researchers find the true meaning of lived experiences, usually hidden or distorted (Van Manen, 1990).

Third, the phenomenological method differs from traditional research in that traditional research specifies beforehand what it predicts the research to reveal. Van Manen (1990) describes phenomenological human science as discovery-oriented. Phenomenological questions are "meaning questions"—questions that ask for the possible meaning and significance of a certain phenomenon (Van Manen, 1990). According to Marcel (1950), "meaning questions" cannot be resolved and thus done away with; instead, the essence of such questions is the opening and keeping open of possibilities (Gadamer, 1975).

Fourth, phenomenology seeks to study phenomena in an open, unconstrictive way. Ambiguity is viewed as productive, necessary, and valuable (Lanigan, 1979). Through the process of bracketing and imaginative free variation (viewing the phenomena with and without essential themes), an openness can be achieved that allows inquiry to be free of structure (Nelson, 1989b) and representative of true lived experiences. In this sense, research is not reported via preconceived notions of clearly stated hypotheses but inductively in terms of the descriptive lived experiences to which the person gives consciousness.

Fifth, phenomenology is interested in the study of "persons," as opposed to "individuals" (Van Manen, 1990). Primarily a biological word, *individuals* can refer to any number of things: an animal, an organism, a plant, and so on. But according to Auden (1967), the word *person* describes the uniqueness of each human being. Furthermore, phenomenological studies do not involve "subjects" as does traditional empirical research. The persons involved in the research project are called "participants," "narrators" (Gluck & Patai, 1991), or more recently, "co-researchers" (Ford-Ahmed, 1992; Orbe, 1993, 1994b). This shift in terminology does not simply represent a more politically correct language but also reflects the way in which researchers approach their inquiry. Such a distinction in language is important because the terms shape the way in which co-researchers view themselves (Etter-Lewis, 1991). In this regard, persons can be viewed as multidimensional and complex and from a particular social, cultural, and historical life circumstance (Van Manen, 1990).

Finally, phenomenology focuses on researching conscious experience (capta) rather than hypothetical situations (data) (Lanigan, 1979). *Capta* refers to what is taken from experience and allows people to assign meaning to themselves. *Data,* on the other hand, refers to what is given and the collection process involves gathering information from participants by which interviewers find meaning via a preset agenda. With phenomenology, researchers view the co-researchers as human beings who signify—give meaning to and derive meaning from—their world (Van Manen, 1990). Phenomenologists are active in becoming a medium for the voice of their co-researchers without necessarily manipulating, altering, or reshaping their life experiences (Gluck & Patai, 1991).

In short, phenomenology represents a philosophic and human science research method (Nelson, 1989a) that studies the lived experiences of persons while remaining sensitive to the uniqueness of the person (Van Manen, 1990). Highly synergistic in nature, this qualitative method rigorously seeks to assign meaning to phenomena. Lanigan (1979, 1988) and others (Nelson, 1989b; Peterson, 1987) outline three steps in a phenomenological framework—description, reduction, and interpretation—that strive toward this objective. The first step in a phenomenological inquiry is gathering descriptions of lived experiences. Nevertheless, before this process, researchers must give consciousness to their subjective position with the phenomena.

Phenomenological Description

Phenomenology is grounded in and begins with the lived experience of the researcher involved in the study (Daley, 1978). Phenomenologists must draw on their lived experiences to gain insight into the phenomenon that is the focus of their research. A self-assessment by the researcher is a crucial first step in a phenomenological study because it allows the researcher to become aware of his or her preconceived biases, ideas, and subjectivity. It also serves to identify the researcher as a person with a historical, social, and personal identity (Erni, 1989).

Erni cites the importance of this self-assessment as crucial in the process of self-reflexivity. A researcher's positioning must be acknowledged and articulated as it functions within the social and power structures and viewed as a significant element in phenomenological research. Only by consciously involving oneself with this process can researchers begin to bracket their conscious experience when the phenomenological description, collection, and transcription begin (Lanigan, 1979).

Nelson (1989b) further describes this starting point as helpful in formulating a process of "intuitive reasoning which is neither haphazard nor illogical, but . . . instantiates an abducting, situational logic" (p. 222). Self-reflexivity, according to Minister (1991), is not only legitimate but inseparable from the phenomenological method.

Recently, phenomenologists in the field of communication effectively gathered descriptions of lived experience by using a combination of the open-ended and general interview guide approach (Patton, 1983). This approach allows a more spontaneous exchange, resulting in more freedom and flexibility for researchers and co-researchers (Anderson & Jack, 1991). It is important to remember that the researcher's role is to foster freedom of description by the co-researcher and to avoid the imposition of personal expectations stated in the interview topical (Heilbrun & Stimpson, 1975). Three specific phenomenological techniques communication researchers use to study lived experiences are in-depth interviews, focus group discussion, and critical incidents. The research leading to the development of co-cultural theory (Ford-Ahmed & Orbe, 1992; Orbe, 1994b, in press; Roberts & Orbe, 1996) included multiple uses of the techniques described below.

In-Depth Interview

The most commonly used approach to collect capta in phenomenological inquiries is through in-depth interviews. Interviews are a valuable tool for collecting descriptions of lived experiences of co-researchers because they allow them to tell their stories in their own words (Anderson & Jack, 1991). For phenomenological studies, in-depth interviews are only effective when researchers can create a topical protocol of general, open-ended questions that allow each co-researcher to inductively explore topical areas that represent salient issues in her or his own experiences. The issues and hypothetical questions included in the topical protocol are used only when co-researchers are unable to continue to describe their lived experiences related to the phenomenon. In this regard, phenomenological interviews are different from those used in traditional research, which typically use a standard, preconceived set of questions for each interview.

Focus Group Discussions

Focus group discussions present another opportunity for phenomenologists to collect descriptions of lived experiences. The purpose of focus groups is to gather capta by which co-researchers can consider their own views in the context of the views of others (Patton, 1983). Focus groups are typically used because they not only provide a time-efficient method to draw on several persons' experiences at once; they also create a context that encourages synergistic insights unattainable during individual interviews (Cooks & Orbe, 1993). Besides group dynamics contributing to the descriptions of lived experiences (Patton, 1983), focus groups organized into homogeneous clusters also appear uniquely appropriate for co-cultural communication research since in-group peers typically play a central role in social constructions of reality and identity formation.

Furthermore, focus groups can be used toward the latter stages of research studies to gather perceptions about outcomes and consequences (Patton, 1983). Van Manen (1990) suggests that focus groups operate in a hermeneutic sense in that researchers can reflect with co-researchers on the topic at hand. This additional step in the gathering process shows the role that co-researchers play in phenomenological studies. In contrast to traditional research, in which data are collected from participants and the relationship ends, focus group participants can attempt to interpret, modify, and enhance the contributions of others (Minister, 1991). Van Manen (1990) concludes that these hermeneutic focus groups "are helpful in generating deeper insights and understandings. . . . Thus themes are examined, articulated, reinterpreted, omitted, added, or reformulated" (p. 100).

Critical Incident

One method used sparingly, yet effectively, to gather phenomenological descriptions of lived experiences is the critical incident technique (Orbe, 1994b). This method, initially described by Flanagan (1954), is one way to get at the co-researchers' perspective on their lived experiences (Patton, 1983). Several communication scholars have used this psychologically based method (Biles, Shapiro, & Cummings, 1988; Kreps, 1991), as well as a few phenomenological studies (e.g., Leslie, 1997). The use of this research method for communication research appears consistent with Pennington's (1979) call for increased use of critical incidents in research on culture and communication.

The basic strategy behind the critical incident technique is to ask co-researchers to describe a past communication interaction (Flanagan, 1954). Consistent with the inductive approaches of the interview and focus group discussion, collecting critical incidents successfully allows co-researchers to describe self-selected events of significance from their own perspectives. The process for gathering and interpreting descriptions, as described by Kreps (1991), is consistent with the assumptions and processes for phenomenological studies.

Minister (1991) suggests that researchers urge co-researchers explicitly to place themselves in a subjective position within the research study so that a productive dialogic relationship will be established. The ultimate goal of gathering phenomenological descriptions is to create a discursive space where co-researchers are provided an opportunity to tell their stories in their own terms (Anderson & Jack, 1991). Such an environment will result in "good" phenomenological descriptions. As delineated by Van Manen (1990), "A good phenomenological description is collected by lived experience and recollects lived experience—is validated by lived experience and validates lived experience" (p. 27).

Finally, researchers must follow three guidelines while gathering phenomenological descriptions (Ihde, 1977). First, researchers must attend to phenomena of experience as they reveal themselves. This guideline coincides with the processes of bracketing and imaginative free variation described earlier in this chapter. Second, researchers and co-researchers should focus on describing and not explaining the phenomena. Although the temptation to interpret and explain phenomena will undoubtedly be present, phenomenological researchers must focus on collecting detailed, vivid descriptions of the lived experiences of their co-researchers. Third, phenomenologists should initially horizontalize all descriptions; in other words, each characterization should be viewed as equally important. Interview protocols and research questions must be bracketed so that no one set of descriptions is distinguished as more important than others.

Phenomenological Reduction

The co-researchers' descriptions of their lived experiences serve as fundamental recollections that the researcher typically logs via tape recordings and then onto written transcripts (Nelson, 1989b). The process of transcribing interviews is important in phenomenological reduction because it represents an opportunity to become more aware of the phenomenon as consciously described by co-researchers (Nelson, 1989a). Through this process, transcripts begin to "speak" to researchers, and themes, which are essential to the phenomena, begin to emerge from the text.

Thematizations

The ultimate goal of a phenomenological reduction is to determine which parts of the description are essential and which are not (Lanigan, 1979); this objective requires seeking out the structural features of the phenomenon (Ihde, 1977). The researcher reflects on the descriptions offered by the co-researchers to specify the structuring of their lived realities (Nelson, 1989b). The second phenomenological step of reduction also represents an opportunity for researchers to bring together and analyze the transcriptions and begin to refine, expand, develop, and discard themes, concepts, and ideas.

A thematic phrase at best represents a simplification. Van Manen (1990) describes it as a way to give "shape to the shapeless" (p. 88), by pointing at, alluding to, or hinting at one aspect of the phenomenon. The phenomenological reduction consists of abstracting words and phrases from the transcripts that function as existential signifiers (Colaizzi, 1973) or revelatory phrases (Nelson, 1989a, 1989b).

One method for creating themes is described as the selective reading approach (Van Manen, 1990). Researchers involve themselves with and become closer to the lived experiences of the co-researchers and must ask themselves, "What statement(s) or phrase(s) seem particularly essential or revealing about the phenomenon or experience being described" (Van Manen, 1990, p. 93)?

The goal of the phenomenologist here, in contrast to traditional empirical researchers, is not to create a consensus about lived experiences but to concern herself or himself with the essential structures of the lived experience as lived logic (Colaizzi, 1973). Researchers must ask themselves, Which parts of the co-researchers' lived experiences are truly part of their consciousness as opposed to those that are merely assumed (Lanigan, 1979)? The process of imaginative free variation assists in accomplishing this task.

Imaginative Free Variation

Imaginative free variation is crucial to accomplishing a phenomenological reduction (Lanigan, 1979). This method consists of reflecting on the aspects of the co-researchers' lived experiences that are conscious, affective, and cognitive and systematically imagining each aspect present or absent within the lived experience (Lanigan, 1979). By comparing and contrasting these aspects, phenomenological researchers can determine which themes are essential in the lived experiences of their co-researchers. Incidental or happenstance themes are eliminated during this procedure (Van Manen, 1990); such initial interpretations are supported or refuted by co-researchers during subsequent focus group discussions. Nelson (1989b) describes the process of imaginative free variation in this way:

> Through the techniques of imaginative free variation, which contextualizes various features of the phenomenon within the whole, and

> which allows for comparison and contrast, a pattern of experience emerges. With it emerges the shape of the phenomenon as it is attended to in experience. (p. 235)

Thematizations represent a reduction of the descriptions generated by co-researchers (Van Manen, 1990). Nevertheless, it is important to note that the descriptions become strictly thematic only reflectively (Nelson, 1989b). Phenomenologists use an intentional process of reflection to attempt to capture the essence of the phenomenon. The end result of this reduction is the emergence of several themes that assist in giving "shape to the shapeless" (Van Manen, 1990, p. 88). To allow these themes to emerge, several steps of review are employed.

Reduction Process

The first step in a phenomenological reduction is the transcription of co-researchers' lived experiences. To review each transcript "horizontally" each piece of information should be dealt with individually. The first step is to read each transcript without making any notations; this is an important process by which researchers can refamiliarize themselves with the descriptions of lived experiences. The next step involves reading the transcript a second time and highlighting words, phrases, and recollections that emerge as essential in the lived experiences of the co-researchers. The final step in this process is to bracket these paradigmatic (initial) thematizations from the first transcript before beginning the same process for other transcripts. As each transcript is sure to produce several initial thematizations, researchers must work consciously to bracket these ideas in order to approach each transcript horizontally.

Once this initial reduction process is completed, a second review of all transcripts and initial thematizations is completed to become more familiar with the initial findings. This review typically produces many possible themes. A third review (using imaginative free variation) of the transcripts and general themes typically reveals that several themes are interconnected, redundant (therefore combined under a more general heading), or incidental. Incidental themes, not essential to the lived experiences of the phenomenon, are subsequently eliminated. This intermediate level of thematization reduces the large number of initial thematizations, more general (and generic) in nature, to major themes that seem to reveal the essence of the transcripts.

Phenomenological Interpretation

The third step in phenomenological method is interpretation (also described as hermeneutic analysis; Lanigan, 1979; Polkinghorne, 1983). Nelson (1989b) describes this step as one that attempts to discover the interrelatedness among the themes that link the phenomenon under investigation with consciousness. Furthermore, the goal of a phenomenological interpretation is to find the meanings that were not immediately apparent in the earlier steps (Spiegelberg, 1960/1982). Merleau-Ponty (1968) refers to this operation as "hyper-reflection."

This process begins by reviewing the essential themes and formulating ideas of how these themes relate to one another (syntagmatic thematization). Merleau-Ponty (1968, p. 38) uses "hyper-reflection" to refer to an interpretation that incorporates its findings (and how this interpretation affects the phenomenon) and then reexamines the initial interpretation. According to Nelson (1986), hyper-reflection is a process "which takes itself and the changes that it introduces into the phenomenon into further account" (p. 134). In this sense, reflexivity, which is present at every stage of a phenomenological inquiry, is distinguished from ordinary introspection (Nelson, 1989b). The process of simultaneously thematizing, bracketing, interpreting, and then beginning the process again (syntagmatic thematization) is described by Nelson (1989b) as a hermeneutic spiral.

Within this reexamination of the interpretive process, one seemingly significant phrase will emerge and serve to interconnect all of the essential themes drawn from the co-researchers' descriptions of their lived experiences. Although often first passed by or discarded as unimportant, these relevant phrases manage to tap the essence of the phenomenon under investigation.

The most important lesson of this process is the impossibility of a complete reduction or interpretation (Merleau-Ponty, 1948/1962). The intersubjective nature of our interpretations, as de Lauretis (1984) puts it, is "an ongoing construction, not a fixed point of departure or arrival from which one then interacts with the world" (p. 159). Because researchers are consciously engaged in their own lifeworlds and this involvement is an ongoing, dynamic process (Nelson, 1989b), our interpretations change the instant that we view the "finished" product and begin to reflect on it.

The three steps in phenomenological method—description, reduction, and interpretation—represent an interpretive approach to studying the lived experiences of others. The method helps researchers gain understanding of everyday occurrences as they reveal the essential structures of the lived experiences of others. The goal of phenomenological research, as articulated by Nelson (1989b), is to take these critical discoveries and return them to the lifeworld in which we live to increase understanding of human communication.

Phenomenology and Co-cultural Communication Research

Phenomenological inquiries allow an inductive approach to studying communication processes, representing a methodological framework that acknowledges the lived experiences of others. As described throughout this chapter, communication scholars have used phenomenology to facilitate research in a variety of areas. Nevertheless, the tenets of a phenomenological methodology approach seem especially productive for research grounded in muted-group and standpoint theory. Wallace and Wolf (1995) make this affinity explicit when they describe standpoint theory as similar to "phenomenologists who view the realities of women's nature, needs, role, and place in society as systems of ideas constructed in past interactions and sustained by present ongoing interaction" (pp. 270-271).

A phenomenological framework seems particularly suitable for scholars who research the communication processes of co-cultural group members. Whereas culture and communication research has been criticized for producing stereotypical group generalizations (e.g., Orbe, 1995), key phenomenological assumptions (discussed earlier) establish an important vantage point from which advances in research beyond group classifications can occur.

Such scholarly headway can be accomplished due to several advantages when cultural researchers use a phenomenological lens to examine the communication processes of others. First, phenomenology allows researchers to acknowledge and subsequently bracket their preconceived subjective biases while inductively arriving at thematic interpretations. Furthermore, Van Manen's (1990) "meaning questions" encourage an inductive explication of essential communicative features not possible through traditional empirical research methodologies. In this regard, attention to the lived experiences of co-researchers is recognized as confirmation of the vast standpoints within different cultural groups.

Second, through phenomenology, the voices of "muted" group members now can be invited into the research process at each level of inquiry. Phenomenological inquiries that include interviews and focus group discussions gain from co-cultural experiences that hinge on oral rather than written tradition. In this sense, phenomenology constitutes an avenue in scholarly research designed to promote the voices of its co-researchers, which makes it especially pertinent for communication research involving co-cultural group members whose voices have historically been muted in communication research and theory (Gonzalez et al., 1994). Although the advantages articulated earlier are especially relevant for culture and communication studies, they can provide similar benefits for other communication research as well.

Use of this rigorous human science approach encourages an epistemological balance under which specific human lived experiences are the original vantage point for scholarly inquiry. This fundamental idea of phenomenological inquiry is crucial for research that questions dominant-based ideologies, challenges culturally learned ideas, and treats as problematic what is taken for granted in attempts to gain additional understanding of our everyday world (Wallace & Wolf, 1995). Such efforts also appear to meet the summons for research that acknowledges the specific case, as much as the general tendency (Houston, 1989) and urgent calls for more qualitative methods to increase understanding of complex communication processes (Hecht et al., 1989).

The theoretical framework presented in this book is the product of an inductive exploration of how co-cultural group members communicate within dominant societal structures. It is important to note that the research leading up to the emergence of a co-cultural communication theory is grounded in an epistemology explicit in phenomenology and has gained from the use of its methodological approaches (as explained earlier in the chapter). In fact, the conceptualization presented in the next few chapters can be considered another point of self-reflexivity inherent in the ongoing process of a phenomenological inquiry. This theoretical framework draws from a growing body of existing research on the communication processes involving a number of co-cultural group members. Although this research represents a variety of disciplines and methodological approaches, the fundamental concepts of the theory are grounded in four recent phenomenological research projects involving a total of 89 diverse co-cultural group members from across the country. The findings of each study have been reported previously (Ford-Ahmed & Orbe, 1992; Orbe, 1994b, in press; Roberts & Orbe, 1996). Nevertheless, an infinite process of self-reflexivity promotes a reexamination of these findings and attempts to generate new insight into co-cultural communication.

Unbeknownst to its authors, the crude beginnings of the co-cultural theoretical framework were initiated in the *Qualitative Research Methods* graduate seminar at Ohio University, where I was one of two students who collaborated on a paper exploring the communicative experiences of African American graduate students (Ford-Ahmed & Orbe, 1992). The paper, *African American Graduate Students, Their Majority Host Institution, and Ethnic Prejudice: A Bright Side?* was the result of nine in-depth interviews with African American graduate students conducted early in 1992. The phenomenological infrastructure of this initial research inquiry served as the foundation for my dissertation on African American male communication, which is based on capta gleaned from focus group discussions, in-depth interviews and critical incidents from 35 African American men in 1993. This endeavor (*"Remember, It's Always Whites' Ball": Descriptions of African American Male Communication;* Orbe, 1994b) is the primary source of inspiration for the conceptualization of co-cultural communication theory. Even as I concluded writing the final pages of my dissertation, the idea of exploring the "communicative cultures" of other underrepresented groups was made apparent (Orbe, 1993):

> First, I wonder if this "culture" is unique to African American men. Do African American women function within a similar cultural system? What are the differences, if any, as compared to African American men? The second question that arose concerning culture was in regards to other oppressed groups in our society. I am intrigued to explore how other underrepresented groups—Native Americans, gays and lesbians, and women for example—create communication

> strategies and coping mechanisms to function in an oppressive society. (p. 141)

This point of inquiry was explored during the summer of 1994 when 27 people of color, gays, lesbians, bisexuals, women, and those from a lower socioeconomic status were included in a research project on co-cultural communication (Orbe, in press). Whereas the studies on African American men served as the initial stimulus for this larger endeavor, *Laying the Foundation for Co-cultural Communication Theory: An Inductive Approach to Studying "Non-dominant" Communication Strategies and the Factors that Influence Them* made the relationship between culture, power, and communication clear enough for a theoretical framework to develop. Finally, my involvement in a recent research project on gay men, initiated by a graduate student, also contributed to the evolution of this theory. Roberts and Orbe's (1996) *"Creating That Safe Place Among Family": Exploring Intergenerational Gay Male Communication* involved researching the lived experiences of 18 older and younger gay men (fall 1994-fall 1995).

In summary, this chapter explained the fundamental assumptions and processes of phenomenology and demonstrated its applicability to co-cultural communication research. As evidenced by recent research (Ford-Ahmed & Orbe, 1992; Orbe, 1994b, in press; Roberts & Orbe, 1996), the tenets of this methodology represent a valuable infrastructure for researchers who investigate the intricate relationship between culture and human communication. Subsequent chapters describe the collective insight generated by such an approach and offer an explication of the communicative experiences of co-cultural group members.

Chapter 4

Co-cultural Communicative Practices

As described earlier, co-cultural communication refers to interactions between "dominant" and "nondominant" groups. Co-cultural communication is preferred to other terms (such as *sub-cultured, subordinate,* or *muted group*) since existing terminology connotes co-cultural groups as inferior to dominant group members and passively muted by oppressive communication structures. Since this chapter focuses on a variety of communicative practices that co-cultural group members engage in when interacting with dominant group members, this change in terminology is important as it recognizes their active and adaptive styles of dealing with attempts to mute their voices. Nonetheless, before these co-cultural practices can be identified and explained, it is important to define and describe co-cultural communication for co-cultural group members.

Defining Co-cultural Communication

The definition of co-cultural communication just given is a general one that is easy to understand. Nevertheless, communication between "dominant" and "nondominant" group members is a simplistic definition, given that societal positions consist of simultaneous memberships within a multitude of co-cultural groups. In this regard, the general definition is accurate but problematic since people, such as African American men, can concurrently be dominant (male) and nondominant (African American) group members. Most of the descriptions and strategies in this chapter draw from instances in which co-cultural group members interact with dominant group members—those persons who are European American, male, heterosexual, able-bodied, and/or from the middle or upper socioeconomic status. Nevertheless, other interactions are characterized by two co-cultural group members communicating (e.g., two Puerto Rican women) and another co-cultural variable becomes a salient issue (e.g., one woman's lesbianism) within the interaction.

This is an important consideration as it relates to the idea that people can function as both the "target and vehicle" (Foucault, 1979) of oppressive communication. The stance of dominant group status (e.g., heterosexuality) is pervasive throughout our society. Nevertheless, the positioning of dominant and nondominant group status is also contingent on other co-cultural identities and the specific communication context. For instance, heterosexual women are the target of masculine oppression *but also* may be the vehicle for oppression in their relationships with lesbians. As confirmation to the complex statuses that affect interpersonal communication (ultimately affected by our cultural historicity), instances of such multileveled co-cultural group positions are prevalent throughout this book.

To clarify this phenomenon, the phrase "co-cultural oppression" denotes those behaviors of co-cultural group members that oppress other co-cultural group members. The existence of co-cultural oppression is documented in the existing literature as evidenced by Hull, Scott, and Smith's (1982) attention to the sexism and racism facing African American women, and Luna's (1989) work on "gay racism." Collins (1990) confirms this phenomenon by acknowledging that all persons possess varying amounts of "penalty and privilege" (p. 172). Throughout the recent research leading up to this publication, other examples of co-cultural oppression were evident. For instance, narratives indicating varying levels of classism within the gay community were described in great detail. This clarification is presented to give the reader a more thorough understanding of the complex intricacies behind a seemingly simple idea like co-cultural communication. Now that a definition has been explicated, descriptions of co-cultural communication—for co-cultural group members—can give greater insight into this communication phenomena.

Describing Co-Cultural Communication

Typically, co-cultural group members—despite different personal identities—characterize their communication with dominant group members in fairly consistent terms. Although this is not true for all co-cultural group members, most often they describe their interactions with dominant group members as "cautious," "guarded," "fearful," "quiet," "uncomfortable," "not as outgoing," "careful," and "stifled." Without using specific academic terminology, co-cultural group members describe attempts to have their voices "muted" in different (but not necessarily all) situations. Several oral narratives included in recent research recount instances in which dominant group members would silence co-cultural group members. For instance, one young woman characterizes her experience in a community meeting with other older men (and a few older women) as, "I felt awkward [during discussion]. I had a difficult time getting in a word edgewise. Usually I had to interrupt four or five times until I could speak. . . . It's just very frustrating." Without question, co-cultural group members often feel "stifled" by persons representing more powerful (dominant) groups. The cause of their muteness varies—age, ethnicity, gender, affection or sexual orientation, or socioeconomic status—but hinges on their perceived powerlessness and outgroup positioning in different situations.

The adjectives just offered indicate that many co-cultural group members are involved in a process of "conscious communication" when interacting with dominant group members. Instead of the spontaneous interaction typical of intracultural communication, co-cultural group members are apprehensive while speaking with others unlike themselves and "careful to say exactly what [they] mean."

One 32-year-old European American gay man describes his interaction with his European American heterosexual boss in these words, "I feel maybe every word that I'm saying is being scrutinized." The same man characterizes his behavior with dominant group members as a "performance on front stage"; such a description also seems appropriate for an African American woman who feels that associates are "evaluating me all the time." The experiences of other co-cultural group members appear to mirror these perceptions. Clearly, they have learned that interacting freely with persons unlike themselves can be counterproductive and ultimately dangerous. The explanation that a Hispanic woman offered seems to capture a lot of the sensations experienced by different co-cultural group members:

> What I found in communicating with [a European American male supervisor], was that you, of course, could not express yourself freely. You were totally in a subordinate position and therefore a little intimidated and afraid of the consequences for being honest.

For co-cultural group members, the need for strategic communication is reinforced by instances in which they did attempt to have their voices heard, only to be ignored by others. For co-cultural group members, differences based on levels of societal power attributed to various co-cultures made intergroup communication sometimes difficult. The following assertions were articulated by different persons but focus on a common theme (in each case, "he" refers to a European American male colleague or acquaintance): "He simply wouldn't listen; he was simply refusing to communicate with me" (Hispanic woman). "It's just that he didn't listen" (African Native American man). "He didn't listen to me—he just blew me off!" (European American woman). A Filipino European American woman's description of her interaction with another biethnic (African Latino) man elucidates the notion of "co-cultural oppression":

> He doesn't hear me, and if he would just listen he would realize what my point was. But he is just too busy talking all the time, so he never hears my point. He has already got it made up in his mind what I'm going to say . . . before I even say it. It's not just me, it's all women.

These descriptions characterize interactions with dominant group members in many settings: work, school, home, social, and public.

Narratives recount blatant power plays as illustrated above, but co-cultural group members also experience more subtle forms of oppressive forces, "things that you just can't name." These instances typically occur in environments that appear to be receptive to diverse voices. But as one Mexican American man shares, whenever a person has begun to let his or her guard down, something occurs that brings back feelings of disappointment, frustration, and introspection. "It [a nonchalant racist remark] surprised me and saddened me. Just little comments like that are being said all the time. . . . Why? What is the significance of those little comments?" An African American woman whose visit home was disrupted when she displayed some affection for her lesbian lover illustrates that even "home" is not safe from oppressive overtures. As she succinctly put it, "That shit hurts. They're supposed to be my family." Even when co-cultural group members want to eliminate the protective barriers constructed around them, the process is often not an easy one. One African American faculty member shares that some "white" colleagues

> tell me that I think too much. . . . "Let it out, speak your mind," [they tell me]. But I've developed this habit and you know that habits die hard, so I haven't been able to do that yet.

The depiction of co-cultural communication portrayed here represents one that is highly stressful, exhausting, and consequential. Although a few co-cultural members attempted to isolate themselves in homogeneous settings ("I just said the heck with it and moved" or "I ended up getting transferred"), they ultimately recognize that some interaction with dominant group members is unavoidable, given societal structures. Reflecting this reality, co-cultural group members adopted specific communicative practices to survive or succeed in environments created (and are largely maintained) with structures that are oppressive.

Explicating Communicative Practices

The focus of this chapter is on the identification and explanation of various communicative practices that co-cultural group members report using while interacting within dominant societal structures.

These practices do not represent a fixed state of communication for co-cultural group members; instead, their communicative behaviors are a negotiation that interacts with dominant group members (Spradlin, 1995). Communication is a bidirectional, dialectic, transactional process and the communicative practices explicated in this chapter describe the perceptions of this process for co-cultural group members. The use of gerunds (-ing) to describe the practices that co-cultural group members use while functioning in dominant group structures reflects that these communicative behaviors typically emerge through interactions with others. The objective of listing and describing this initial assortment of communicative practices is not to create a series of mutually exclusive tactics but to present specific communicative behaviors as described throughout recent co-cultural communication research. To this end, some communicative practices may seem to overlap or contradict other practices.

With one or two exceptions, the practices included here were described by a diverse group of co-researchers in several recent research projects (Ford-Ahmed & Orbe, 1992; Orbe, 1994b, in press; Roberts & Orbe, 1996). Specific narratives are included to illustrate each communicative practice. Unless otherwise noted, these illustrations were shared by co-researchers in recent phenomenological research by Orbe and colleagues. A total of 26 co-cultural practices is described: (a) avoiding, (b) averting controversy, (c) maintaining interpersonal barriers, (d) emphasizing commonalities, (e) exemplifying strengths, (f) mirroring, (g) dissociating, (h) dispelling stereotypes, (i) manipulating stereotypes, (j) embracing stereotypes, (k) developing positive face, (l) censoring self, (m) extensive preparation, (n) overcompensating, (o) communicating self, (p) educating others, (q) intragroup networking, (r) strategic distancing, (s) ridiculing self, (t) using liaisons, (u) increasing visibility, (v) confronting, (w) gaining advantage, (x) bargaining, (y) attacking, and (z) sabotaging others.

Avoiding

One communicative practice that co-cultural group members engage in while functioning in a dominant environment is avoidance. As reported by Ribeau, Baldwin, and Hecht (1994), this strategy can include avoiding a person, conversation, or topics. In this framework two forms are described: *avoiding* and *averting controversy.* Avoiding is more physical in nature and involves co-cultural group members who acknowledge "maintaining a distance" with acquaintances and co-workers. Others clearly communicate only with people different from themselves when absolutely necessary. African American men, for instance, discuss how they practice "social avoidance": avoiding places and gatherings where they would be expected to talk with them (here referring to European American men). Persons from a lower socioeconomic background express similar attempts to avoid social gathering places where "uppity people hang out."

Elijah Anderson, a sociology professor at the University of Pennsylvania, describes "Type A" and "Type B" middle-class African Americans. Type A African Americans, according to Anderson (1990), avoid interacting with European Americans; in addition (Hamilton, 1996), "For Type A, race comes first. They tend not to associate with whites unless it is necessary and are intolerant of blacks who do mix freely" (p. A4). Hamilton describes two African American attorneys who can be characterized as Type A. Living in an African American suburb of Atlanta, Georgia, the couple "run[s] a budget legal center in a poor black Atlanta neighborhood. They don't have white friends and, unless they go to court, they rarely see white faces" (p. A4).

Avoiding is also seen in segregation behaviors. D'Souza (1991) uses the term "ethnic enclaves" (p. 21) that are apparent for different co-cultural groups. Residual housing, which includes neighborhoods essentially divided by ethnicity, sexual orientation, or socioeconomic status are typically the means to and result of physical avoidance.

Averting Controversy

Whereas avoiding involves maintaining a certain level of tangible distance between co-cultural group members, averting controversy consists of deflecting communication away from topics that deal with certain "controversial" or potentially dangerous subject areas. In this regard, people of color may abstain from discussions about affirmative action, O. J. Simpson, or California's Proposition 187. Women may use topic shifts and other practices to deflect potential conversations on sexism, the glass ceiling, or other topics that may cause some friction between men and women. Although co-cultural group members employ this practice in many contexts (social, personal, school), it seems to be especially prevalent at work. One young gay man explains his attitude while in the office, "I don't get involved too much. . . . They will have these conversations . . . but I don't get involved because I don't want to lead them on one way or the other [concerning his closeted identity]."

Spradlin (1995), writing from a lesbian perspective, uses the word *dodging* (p. 7) to describe this phenomenon. Whereas she reports that lesbians often avert controversy to maintain a closeted identity and "to steer conversation away from personal inquiry" (p. 7), other co-cultural group members employ the tactic to allow dominant group members to escape a certain degree of discomfort. Others reveal that they may engage in superficial dialogue but avoid ever discussing certain "hot" topics (regarding ethnicity, sexuality, etc.) that may lead to offensive remarks. A potently charged topic, such as welfare reform, may be avoided by a variety of co-cultural group members (on the basis of socioeconomic status, sex, or ethnicity) since experiences tell these persons that the discussion usually results in offensive slurs about cultural stereotypes and strained social divisions. Averting controversy, or topical avoidance, can be viewed as a proactive communicative practice distinguishable from a more reactive practice of "censoring self," discussed later.

Maintaining Interpersonal Barriers

Related to the idea of avoiding is the mechanism by which co-cultural group members maintain existing interpersonal barriers to reduce the chances of face-to-face communication with dominant group members. Typically, persons use interpersonal barriers to create and maintain a psychological distance when physical distancing is impossible; such activity draws from the natural tendency for separation between co-cultural groups. For instance one woman described her experiences with a co-worker:

> On several occasions, he has said inappropriate things. So, even when I have to sit next to him in a meeting or something—and this is usually because there are no chairs left—I don't make eye contact or position my body so that we'll have to make any small talk.

With this communicative practice, people use different nonverbal behaviors (space, eye contact, body language) to avoid co-cultural interaction. Whereas topical avoidance typically employs verbal topic shifts to avert discussions, to maintain privacy or an environment relatively free of conflict, this co-cultural practice uses different nonverbal cues. Co-cultural group members could create and maintain barriers—and consequently discourage communication—through a myriad of nonverbal tactics: averting eye contact, maintaining a closed or defensive body position, and/or orchestrating the physical elements in the environment to inhibit interpersonal communication. Such behaviors clearly communicate a certain disposition in the office, as evidenced (Woods, 1993) by one gay man who, "by erecting temporal and spatial barriers . . . minimizes the opportunities for . . . contact" (p. 111):

> He has the reputation of being somewhat aloof and enigmatic at work, someone who doesn't attend all the company parties or outings. He is formal with his superiors and has carefully segregated his personal and professional activities, friends, and identities. "I have a limited relationship with my boss," he explains, "which means I don't always get the mentoring I need." (p. 111)

Emphasizing Commonalities

Emphasizing commonalities, as a co-cultural communicative practice, is one that focuses on human similarities while downplaying or ignoring personal (co-cultural) differences. In the narratives of co-cultural group members involved in recent research projects, a clear indication was given that some persons maintain that their communication does not change when communicating with other persons not like them (dominant group members). "I really don't think that I communicate with them any differently; in a perfect world we are all the same," affirms one 20-year-old Native (Oneida) woman. When communicating with heterosexuals, one gay man reports, "I usually don't try to make an issue of it [gayness], one way or another." A lesbian of Filipino descent speaks of her communicative style in similar terms, "I communicate with everyone the same. . . . I don't even think about that stuff [ethnic and sexuality differences]."

The practice of emphasizing commonalities is employed when persons try to promote a utopian society in which "people are people" and cultural differences are not as significant as shared human characteristics. Co-cultural group members focus on these similarities and try to ignore overt or subtle references to varying levels of racism, classism, heterosexism, sexism, and the like. In certain cases, this practice is attempted even in the face of such adversity. "We are all basically the same," asserts one Mexican American young man who went on to explain that although he often feels that European Americans prejudge and stereotype him, he tries not to let it affect his general outlook on life. Instead, he strives to maintain an "idealized communicative stance" by which he can promote the achievement of a society on the basis of equality and justice.

Exemplifying Strengths

The focus of some co-cultural group members' communicative approach within dominant societal structures was on promoting human unity through idealized communication. Nevertheless, at other times, members of co-cultural groups feel that it is just as important to focus their comments on promoting the recognition of co-cultural groups' accomplishments, strengths, and contributions to society. Those co-cultural group members involved in progroup rhetoric feel it a necessary step to counter the pervasive myth that the country's success is the result of dominant group members' contributions. Although the accomplishments of co-cultural group members are often marginalized to the point of insignificance, some persons feel that identifying and emphasizing co-cultural achievements is important to discount the hegemonic systems of dominant group supremacy.

One consequence of exemplifying strengths is increasing the awareness level of dominant group members in regard to their conceptualization of co-cultural life experiences. Nevertheless, it appears that this communicative practice is used primarily to increase the awareness of other co-cultural group members. Information regarding historical contributions and impressive achievements—usually against tremendous odds—is used to "build up the pride" of other co-cultural group members. In addition, self-awareness is instrumental in empowering co-cultural group members, many of whose self-concepts could not escape the negative effects of societal messages that directly or indirectly cast dominant group members as superior (and co-cultural group members, in comparison, as inferior). One Mexican American man describes how exemplifying the strengths of his people resulted in drastic changes in his outlook on life:

> Knowledge is power. Before I learned the history of our struggles, I naively went about my business without any clear direction. . . . After learning about all that Chicanos have accomplished—despite the racist attitudes in this country—I felt as if I had a purpose. Now I think that it's important that other young people learn about their history. . . . It's the key to seeing yourself as important.

As self-affirming as these exemplifying strengths can be, some co-cultural group members find their use of this practice confined by the perceptions of dominant group members. As evidenced by written exchanges on the issue of multiculturalism (e.g., Asante, 1991; Ravitch, 1990), many dominant group members interpret this practice as "antidominant group" or even "reverse discrimination." To avoid the misperception of a separatist stance, some co-cultural group members use progroup rhetoric sparingly during interactions with dominant group members. Others, like the gay man cited in the following, continue to use the practice as a means of engaging dominant group members despite possible repercussions:

> Every chance I get I let my straight co-workers know about gay achievements. My favorite thing is to identify all of the famous people who were gay . . . usually this comes after they have just talked about how much they like them. I love to see their reactions! They usually accuse me of "getting on my soapbox," but it's important for them to get this information.

Mirroring

Whereas emphasizing commonalities focuses on similarities during communication with dominant group members, mirroring represents an integrative communicative practice that recognizes dominant or subordinate group differences and attempts to downplay those differences. Co-cultural group members who engage in this practice consciously attempt to make their co-cultural identities less visible (or totally invisible) and adopt those behaviors and images of the dominant culture. In this regard, members of different co-cultures venture to mirror—reflect to others—the appearance of the dominant culture.

This communicative tactic translates into different things for different co-cultural groups. Many researchers have discussed this phenomenon, commonly called *passing*, as it relates to people of color (e.g., Stanback & Pearce, 1981). Most discussions on passing in this context have referred to instances when people of color have been accepted into the dominant group by denying membership in other ethnic groups thought to be undesirable (Bradshaw, 1992). Many factors affect the ability to pass, including skin color, facial features, body shape and size, and language ability (Orbe & Strother, 1996). Banks (1988) coined the term *ethnic psychological captivity* (p. 23) to refer to extreme instances in which people of color begin to believe themselves to be part of the dominant group. Whereas the ability to pass ranges for different people of color, *mirroring* is a communication strategy commonly invoked as a variation of passing. For instance, African Americans and Latino Americans describe avoiding the use of slang and ethnic idioms and instead, "talk white." In *How to Survive When You're the Only Black in the Office*, McClenney (1987) advises, "English, while not culturally your native language, is your operative and survival language. I strongly suggest that you learn to use it well" (p. 77). Harvey Coleman, author of *Empowering Yourself: The Organizational Game Revealed*, contends that to be an executive you must "dress like, act like, speak like, and be like an executive" (quoted in Wade, 1996, p. B4). This process includes shedding any manifestations that are linked to your ethnic culture and mirroring the appearances of dominant group members.

Mirroring takes on a similar form for women. It's clear that most women do not try to literally pass for men; however, recent research has described processes by which women downplay their femininity and "act, talk, and dress like men" to survive or succeed in corporate America. These efforts include such endeavors as the "Executive Women's Golf League," whose objective is to encourage and support women's participation in golf, to foster working relationships with men away from the office (O'Donnell, 1994). Some women "emulate the traditional model" (Buzzanell, 1994, p. 359) so well that they have been characterized as "bosses from hell" (Sutton & Moore, 1985) who engage in stereotypically masculine behaviors such as unlimited competition, betrayal, and aggressiveness (O'Leary & Ickovics, 1990).

Other co-cultural group members whose life experiences include little education and lower socioeconomic status may have a seemingly easier opportunity to successfully mirror dominant group members with little chance for detection. These persons reportedly "act smarter," "definitely use bigger words," and "try to speak up to others" when interacting with dominant group members. By adopting the dress, speech, and mannerisms of the dominant culture, European American males within this co-cultural group can effectively mirror other European American males. Nevertheless, for many, even this mechanism is not ideal since most feel as if they are constantly involved in impression management and on the verge of being exposed as an "impostor."

According to Bucholtz (1995), gays and lesbians are different from women, people of color, and other co-cultural group members, because they, given the right disguise, can pass as heterosexual. Recent research by Spradlin (1995) contends that lesbians use as many as six different strategies when passing as heterosexual. Although Woods (1993) describes this process of mirroring as "a counterfeiting strategy" (p. xiv), his personal illustration below (within a homophobic work environment) includes Spradlin's substrategies of dissociating, distracting, and deceiving:

> I went to the company singles night and spoke vaguely about past girlfriends. I was conspicuous about my friendships with women. I told (or at least laughed at) the right jokes and didn't say too much about my interest in theater. On a friend's suggestion, I read the sports section of the *New York Times* and at least twice dragged myself to Yankee Stadium. For a time, I even hid a small notepad in my desk on which I scribbled key biographical information about "Heather," a quite imaginary young woman with brains, looks, and the good sense to have dated me in college. Heather had unfortunately moved to Maine. (p. xiv)

Dissociating

One related aspect of successful mirroring is a conscious attempt to avoid any stereotypical behavior generally associated with your co-cultural group. As seen in the example of the gay male professional, persons use this communicative practice (illustrated by refraining from showing too much interest in theater) as an attempt to negate any affiliation with their cultural identity. To "blend in" with the dominant culture, different co-cultural group members avoid different stereotypical behaviors when in the presence of dominant group members.

Some people of color, for instance, make conscious decisions to abstain from certain behaviors that others stereotypically identify with all members of their ethnic group. Recently, an African American woman made it very clear to me that she does not eat watermelon or fried chicken in public, although at home both are regularly consumed. Similarly, Asian Americans and Latino Americans may select foods that are not part of their normal diets—all in attempts to dodge ethnic stereotypes. In similar ways, women may avoid any references to soap operas, personal relationships, or gossip. Many of these co-cultural group members avert stereotypical behaviors as a rule, as seen in the following example of one gay man:

> I try to avoid the issue of sex altogether around straight people, because they usually think that gay men are hung up on sex. . . . I don't like to be really friendly to children, either, for the reason [that] there's a child molester stereotype.

In addition, Woods (1993) reports that many gay men "play against" the stereotypes of gay men by avoiding effeminate behaviors. To this end, their outwardly masculine behaviors are taken as evidence of their heterosexuality by unenlightened dominant group members. "The people in their fifties, unless they know someone specifically, have a stereotype of what a gay person is. I don't equal that stereotype, therefore I'm not gay" (p. 92).

For those who use this communicative practice as a way to mirror dominant society, attempts are also made to avoid stereotypical behaviors that dominant group members may find positive and want to emulate. Asian Americans, for instance, may purposely get Cs (or worse) in math classes not to set themselves apart from other (dominant group) students. Women, against much cajoling, may adamantly refuse to host company dinners at their home—although away from the office they pride themselves on the accomplishments in the kitchen. As illustrated in the following example articulated by an African American man, this strategy is sometimes awkward and even farcical!

> I attended a small private college where I was one of a few African Americans who was not an athlete. During one semester, I decided to rush a white fraternity and was invited to a weekend of events. Although most of the fraternity expected me to enthusiastically jump in and play basketball in a pickup game, I lied and told them that I wasn't very good. That night, during a dance at the house, I played it cool and didn't dance at all. After a lot of coaxing, I finally got on the dance floor and did the best I could *NOT* to dance to the rhythm of the song!

Dispelling Stereotypes

One primary aspect of communication, for members of different co-cultures, is how to deal with cultural stereotypes that obscure dominant group thinking during interactions. One co-cultural practice, as described earlier, is to avoid stereotypes at all costs. Nevertheless, three additional tactics appear feasible: dispelling stereotypes, manipulating stereotypes, and embracing stereotypes. Although these co-cultural communicative practices are closely related, distinctions between them are important to understand.

Whereas dissociating oneself from stereotypes is a conscious and active attempt by co-cultural group members, dispelling stereotypes is a behavior that is largely unconscious and "natural." For some people, this practice is a by-product of being spontaneous, open, and unreserved when in environments populated by dominant group members. It does not refer to instances when individuals purposely go out of their way to contradict cultural stereotypes; instead co-cultural group members find times when their mere presence acts as a means to counter stereotypical beliefs. This more placid approach can be seen in the following comments by a 31-year-old African American lesbian:

> A lot of times people have a certain impression on how black people talk, or lesbians are supposed to act. And just being myself, people are like "Well, you're not what I expected". . . . I found if I am just myself and the fact that I am a black woman, and I am a lesbian, they get to see that all African American women are not on welfare [or] heterosexuals dependent on men.

Typically, cultural stereotypes are the result of a lack of meaningful exposure to different groups. Stereotypic beliefs are maintained through limited (oftentimes inaccurate) information supplied by family, friends, or the media. Once dominant group members meet increased numbers of co-cultural group members, existing stereotypes may then be contrasted with actual behaviors. In this regard, "just being yourself," which includes personal behaviors and characteristics that do not fit cultural generalizations and some that do, assists in the deconstruction of stereotypic beliefs. Dispelling stereotypes, therefore, involves inconspicuously setting a positive example through actions and allowing dominant group members to observe the vast diversity within different cultural groups.

Manipulating Stereotypes

The co-cultural communicative practices of avoiding and dispelling stereotypes represent conscious and unconscious attempts to refute some of the stereotypes that dominant group members assign to different co-cultural groups. Nevertheless, manipulating stereotypes, as a co-cultural communicative practice, does not attempt to challenge existing stereotypes but to exploit them for personal gain. In other words, instead of actively avoiding or inadvertently dispelling "stereotypical" behaviors, some members of co-cultural groups conform to commonly accepted ones to obtain certain benefits. For instance, women may "manipulate men" by strategically crying, flirting, or acting ignorant. Such tactics, in the words of women, are used to get men to "buy you drinks," "do your homework," or "carry heavy items." The "oh-please-I'm-so-helpless" approach, as one woman described it, is an effective method to exploit the negative stereotype held by many men that women are not able to be independent and competent.

Men of color also report engaging in this co-cultural communicative practice. Some modify their behaviors to match the "hot-tempered Latino male" or "angry black man" stereotypes if they notice that dominant group members seem easily intimidated. One African American explained,

> I love it when people are intimidated by my presence. Although I wouldn't hurt a fly, white people automatically assume certain things when they see a big black man. For instance, one time I was checking into a hotel, and I didn't even have to do much more than look at this one guy and he was ready to give me anything I needed!

This practice appears to correspond to *shucking*, a strategy described by Stanback and Pearce (1981). Shucking represents instances when subordinate people act in ways to reinforce stereotypical thinking but cognitively reject the meanings associated with those stereotypes. From this perspective, co-cultural group members exploit the ignorance of dominant group members and selectively manipulate stereotypes to accomplish particular goals.

Embracing Stereotypes

A fourth alternative to dealing with dominant group stereotypes is for co-cultural group members to proudly embrace some stereotypical characteristics as their own. From this perspective, persons from different co-cultural groups undertake a negotiated reading of cultural stereotypes by which they adopt the dominant ideology in broad outline but selectively apply it in specific cases and reject it in others. In this regard, those characterizations that dominant society casts on co-cultural groups as an indication of their "less-than-dominant-group status" is espoused and transposed into something positive for the group.

This co-cultural communicative practice was seen in varying levels in the oral narratives of several co-cultural group members, including those of women, people of color, and gays and lesbians. Often the inclination to embrace cultural stereotypes occurs when the categorization is one that contains positive connotations, despite the negativity associated with promoting gross generalizations on the basis of co-cultural identity. Women may embrace the stereotype of "super-mom," naturally more efficient than fathers at child care and in household duties. Gay men sometimes espouse the "fact" that they, as compared to their heterosexual counterparts, are more enlightened about fashion, design, and color.

One set of comments from an African American man appears to best capture the essence of embracing stereotypes as a co-cultural communicative practice. The central idea associated with this tactic, to assume a negotiated reading on cultural stereotypes grounded in dominant ideologies, is illustrated by a sample of his remarks:

> Whites are always trying to prove the "less-than" status of people of color; of course "less-than" means not like the average white. . . . They

> are always searching our culture for evidence of our inferiority—take our food for example. They say that normal people wouldn't eat chitlins, pig's feet, or whatever . . . and some blacks won't eat those traditional foods because of those perceptions. I eat them with pride! What whites don't understand is that historically blacks have had to make do with what was available—they were able to make great tasting feasts from parts of animals that others simply threw away.

Developing Positive Face

One communicative practice articulated by many co-cultural group members in recent research projects involves being "gracious communicators." Some describe a proficiency at becoming more "respectful," "polite," and "more attentive" when interacting with dominant group members. Women reportedly employ this practice when communicating with men with whom they worked. One 20-year-old woman, when asked about male supervisors, professes, "I am very aware of what their expectations of me are and try to follow them." Another woman describes her interaction with a male supervisor:

> I used respectful communication a lot when I worked in an office with my boss. . . . He is definitely task oriented, dominant, and controlling. It was difficult to work for him, I figured that he deserved a lot of respect . . . plus, if I was extra nice, polite, and respectful, I thought I could get him to like me more.

This form of strategic response centers on *stroking* the ideals of dominant group members while fortifying a subordinate positioning. In other words, co-cultural group members consciously try to assist in the maintenance of "positive face" for dominant group members. According to Brown and Levinson (1978), politeness and other forms of "respectful communication" are often strategies for gaining or maintaining favor. Examples of this communicative practice include attempts to appear less threatening and less assertive to supervisors or co-workers. This could mean strategically using hedges, hesitations, or tag questions (Bradac & Mulac, 1984). For instance, one African Native American man describes developing positive face when interacting with European American co-workers, "I find myself even having to approach them differently, with a softer tone. I have to go in there and really make it seem like it was their (co-worker's) idea . . . to be less of a threat." Other co-cultural group members describe similar power dynamics in a variety of social settings. For instance, one African American woman's experiences when meeting different people at a community reception reflect this tendency:

> It was subtle but undeniable. At this reception, there must have been at least 50 people. . . . I guess that only five or six of us had our Ph.Ds. And although everyone was introducing themselves with first and last names only, this one young white man kept introducing himself as Dr. ______ ______. I thought it was really odd—but then I found myself using his title to introduce him too.

In this instance, the subtle practice of using a formal title when addressing colleagues and friends (while they use more informal greetings) is an example of "developing positive face."

Censoring Self

In the opening section of this chapter, co-cultural group members described their interaction with dominant group members as "very conscious." Besides being very mindful when interacting with others, many persons describe instances when they are extremely offended by dominant group members but decide to remain silent. Instead of confronting the offenders or disclosing their discomfort, they resolve to contain their immediate reactions and "say nothing," "blow it off," or as one person aptly depicted, "swallow it." One European American lesbian woman describes her reaction during some informal conversations about Amendment 2 in Colorado when discussions about gays and lesbians became frequent (Spradlin, 1995):

> I was present in conversations when people stated "what do *they* want, anyway, special rights?" and "what *they* do in their bedroom is their business, but why flaunt it?" I found myself . . . biting my tongue to keep silent. (p. 6)

Many times the decision to monitor reactions is a direct result of the perceived consequences that might follow an honest, open response. A Mexican American man, explaining his reaction to a racial slur (concerning African Americans) made by a professor, put it this way:

> And I'm like, "Why are you telling me that?" So, I look at him and was really going to say something, but I'm a student and maybe I don't want to jump the gun. He's going to be teaching me for the next two years, so I thought "I'm going to listen to it and wait a little bit" . . . okay, fine.

Typically, censoring self occurs when co-cultural group members feel as if their response would magnify cultural differences and/or alienate them from others. Such was the case with one woman who made a decision not to respond to an ignorant comment during a trip to the store with some college friends:

> While standing in line, one of my friends made a nasty remark about a woman in front of us who was using food stamps. I can't stand when people make those types of ignorant comments, but when she looked at me, I just nodded in agreement. At that point, I chose not to tell her that my family had been on welfare.

McClenney (1987) advises that co-cultural group members, to succeed in dominant society, should practice "mental discipline" (p. 99). Specifically, he offers the following recommendation:

> When you disagree with someone else and your gut wants to "get them straight," or "give them a piece of your mind," or "tell the son-of-a-bitch off," stop and think a minute, think about it, ask yourself, "what will I gain by arguing?" (p. 99)

Extensive Preparation

For some co-cultural group members, face-to-face communication with dominant group members is inaugurated only after a great deal of preparation. "I have to think about what I am going to say first," explains one Filipino European woman. The cognitive rehearsal that she depicts is echoed by many others, some of whom describe this tendency as appropriate since they did not want to waste others' time (somewhat related to developing positive face). Some co-cultural group members even take their preparation to the extreme when they find themselves involved in an extensive (over-)preparation process. One African American man, who was involved in a recent research project, professed that when talking with European American men, "I prepare talking with them [so that] I am much more thorough and pointed." One African American woman explained that she meticulously prepares for one-on-one meetings with her direct supervisor so that she can be "careful and precise [and] say exactly what I mean . . . and not waste time." Before the encounter, she asks herself, "What exactly do I want to get across? What will produce these results?" Extensive preparation is seen almost as a necessity for some people who feel relatively powerless in certain situations. This need is described by a 21-year-old European American woman who told the other members of a focus group about her experiences in dealing with some men in a small group project:

> And I realized that I was going to have to talk. . . . I had to go through all of this research . . . so that when I went in there, I was the one doing all of the talking and asking all of the questions.

Another European woman, 53 years of age, was quick to substantiate this idea, "I think that I do that too. I don't like surprises; if something is coming up, I try to cover my bases."

Extensive preparation is a co-cultural communicative practice that some people find necessary, especially as a strategic response to a communicative environment that they characterize as lacking in spontaneous exchange. Instead, some members of co-cultural groups describe communication that is carefully selected, well thought out, and typically focused on task orientation. One need for such dialogue is extensive preparation.

Overcompensating

Extensive preparation, as a co-cultural communicative practice, is typically practiced before face-to-face interactions with dominant group members. Overcompensating, however, is a tactic that is used more consistently when co-cultural group members find themselves interacting regularly with those representing the dominant culture (e.g., Woods, 1993). Most often, this practice is described as a tactic used in different professional, community, or social organizations. Co-cultural group members, typically in response to a pervasive fear of discrimination, find themselves trying to be the "exemplary team player." To this end, they strive to earn the reputation of "hard worker," as the following description from a young woman illustrates:

> I would show up early for work, work off the clock for a while, try to get everything done early, and sometimes even do other people's jobs. This seemed to work fairly well, he [her male supervisor who was known to be harder on female employees] acknowledged that I was a hard worker.

Co-cultural group members who frequently employ overcompensation have accepted the age-old belief that "in order to get half as far, you have to work twice as hard." Therefore, to fit in as an "exemplary team player," some co-cultural group members work diligently to prove that they are as worthy as an organizational member—despite the personal characteristics that some find a detriment. First-generation college students who are from a lower socioeconomic background, for instance, frequently feel that they must employ this strategy to fit in with other college students:

> I feel as if at any point that I am going to be exposed as an impostor—so I make sure to go that extra mile so that the professor and other students see that I have what it takes.

Some use this communicative practice to distinguish themselves from other co-cultural group members, whereas others simply see it as a means for survival. Woods (1993) describes one gay male professional whose organizational livelihood involves constant overcompensation:

> He works long hours and is known for taking the initiative on projects. . . . The aggressive work ethic, [he] says, is just a way of protecting himself. "I run circles around everyone else so no one will ever be able to say I don't outperform anybody in the building. And it's not because I have this great desire to do well. I feel I *have* to outperform everybody. . . . I can't be just okay." (p. 210)

Communicating Self

Whereas some co-cultural group members strive to avoid, dispel, or manipulate stereotypical portrayals, some contend with others' preconceptions by simply being themselves. "I let my accomplishments and personality speak for me," maintains a young Mexican American man in a recent interview. Instead of worrying about the stereotypes that others place on all members of a co-cultural group, these persons do not allow such considerations to affect their behaviors.

Co-cultural group members who exhibit positive self-esteem are likely to be self-assured communicators when interacting with dominant group members. As related to recent research on African American communication (Ribeau et al., 1994), these persons displayed a positive self-presentation (p. 144) by which they feel comfortable in asserting their point of view and constantly remain open, friendly, and genuine. One man of Native (Cochiti) and African American descent explains that this communicative practice at times hinges on permitting one's defenses to become exposed:

> I showed them that I was vulnerable . . . that I was a human being just like they are. . . . I sort of opened up and stripped away all of that exterior stuff and let them see what's inside.

One of the ultimate results of communicating self is the "normalizing the 'abnormal' " (Woods, 1993, p. 180). From the ethnocentric perspective of many dominant group members, co-cultural norms—whether based on ethnicity, socioeconomic status, sexuality, or gender—are viewed as atypical, strange; in essence, "abnormal." For instance, most European Americans have a difficult time understanding many African American cultural norms, such as those related to women's hair care, church worship, styles of conflict, and extended family structure. Those co-cultural group members who employ the practice of communicating self do so to display co-cultural norms as familiar, logical, and mundane. Typically, this is accomplished by highlighting the commonalities of experiences while recognizing the influence of cultural differences. In this regard, co-cultural group members are involved in communication that represents an unfamiliar culture and do so in a way that creates understanding through the display of a universal common experience (life). This process of "making the unusual seem usual" (Woods, 1993, p. 184) is the ultimate result of continued communicating self; however, it is one that is not typically achieved through a conscious attempt to break stereotypical beliefs. Instead, it is a by-product of the presence of those co-cultural group members who strive to be viewed as complex, multidimensional individuals, not simply a member of one co-cultural group.

Educating Others

Whereas some co-cultural group members practice self-assured communication without specific design to enlighten dominant group members, others make educating others a primary objective of their communication. Co-cultural group members often find themselves in an assumed role of "educator," enlightening peers, co-workers, and acquaintances on the aspects of their co-cultural identity. In any number of situations, members of different co-cultures are informally appointed as "community spokesperson" and either directly or indirectly encouraged to offer the "co-cultural perspective" on any given issue. Although this tendency typifies an inclination to commodify co-cultural groups into a generalizable other, some co-cultural group members seize the occasion to share one or many perspectives that might represent the diverse lived experiences of their co-culture. In this regard, they are able to articulate *a* perspective (and not necessarily *the* perspective) that gives dominant group members insight into their communities that was not previously known.

In other circumstances, co-cultural group members take the initiative when "teachable moments," unexpected opportunities for enlightening dominant group members during everyday interactions, present themselves. Simple conversations about holiday celebrations, for instance, allow co-cultural group members to educate dominant group members about Hanukkah, Kwanzaa, or Cinco de Mayo. Some persons, given their atypical accessibility to different organizational settings (something that other co-cultural group members are not usually granted), take the responsibility of educating others as an important aspect of their involvement in dominant environments. The opportunity to educate dominant group members, although sometimes strenuous and laborious, is seen as a crucial step in transposing oppressive environments into places where co-cultural group members have greater access, acceptance, and success. As one 30-year-old Puerto Rican man explains,

> That's why I have started taking advantage of any opportunity that arises. I try to explain everything about us that I can to whites so that younger Puerto Ricans won't have to worry about all of their ignorance as much.

Intragroup Networking

Another way in which co-cultural group members are involved in educating others is during intragroup networking activities. According to many members of various co-cultures, one of the most important communicative practices to engage in while participating in dominant structures is networking with other co-cultural group members. Examples exist throughout co-cultural research by which more experienced co-cultural group members advise younger members on how to function in a society that maintains oppressive practices. Whereas a few people describe associations with members of other co-cultural groups (e.g., an Asian American man networking with a European American woman) in recent research, most focus on the significance of locating other people like themselves for support, encouragement, and inspiration. These individuals are better able to identify with, and subsequently understand, the issues related to functioning in settings that are not representative—nor necessarily supportive—of your co-cultural positioning. As reported by Ray and Miller (1991), networking is a critical venture to dialogue about coping mechanisms, stress, and burnout.

Lipman-Blumen (1988) suggests that "women hold the title for collaborative, contributory, and mentoring behavior" (pp. 24-25). Nevertheless, it appears that women are not the only co-cultural group to engage in this type of highly functional networking behavior. One example is the supportive bond between African Americans, in which "a brother-sister thing exists [and] everyone is family." Described by some as "an intense social responsibility" (Orbe, 1994b, p. 294), African Americans participate in a multigenerational process of assisting younger African Americans toward success. One 43-year-old African American puts it in the following words:

> I recall assorted times when older African Americans—family, friends, and people I didn't even really know—took time to explain certain things about interacting with whites that I didn't understand. I am now trying to pass some of that on.

Strategic Distancing

Although some co-cultural group members find intragroup associations invaluable to their success in dominant society, others adamantly avoid any contact as a means of successfully assimilating in society. This tendency is described in the classic diversity training tool, *A Tale of "O": On Being Different* (Fant et al., 1979). The film describes how those persons in the minority react in majority-dominated environments, one of which is strategic distancing. Persons may avoid associating with other co-cultural group members, the film illustrates, to avoid being pigeonholed as the typical minority group member (i.e., "one of them"). Instead, co-cultural group members use strategic distancing and other communicative practices such as overcompensating to set themselves apart from their counterparts. People of color, for example, may avoid organizations, social gatherings, or meetings that cater solely to intragroup members. One Mexican American college student explained his noninvolvement in a campus organization in these words:

> I didn't want to be seen as only a Mexican American. Instead, I wanted to be regarded as a serious student first and foremost, so I joined other professionally related organizations . . . and not the Latino Business Student Association. Why join organizations that discriminate against those individuals who you are trying to get a job from?

Some co-cultural group members engage in strategic distancing to maintain clear distinctions between themselves and other co-cultural group members in organizational settings (Stockard & Johnson, 1980). Female managers, for instance, may physically and psychologically distance themselves from other women to avoid "being identified as 'one of the girls' " (Slade, 1984, p. 15). A certain personal distance is warranted in maintaining what is deemed as "an appropriate relationship" (O'Leary, 1988, p. 201) between female secretaries and bosses. Other co-cultural group members practice similar behaviors to avoid the assumption that their identity confines them to a certain societal position. One young college student describes her logic behind strategic distancing:

> As a math major I take a lot of classes which have mostly men. In most classes, I find myself sitting right in the middle of a group of men, unconsciously avoiding sitting with other women. I think that by sticking with the men, the professor will not categorize me with the "typical woman," who society says is not supposed to have a mind for math.

Ridiculing Self

Some co-cultural group members adopt an additional communicative practice to achieve strategic distancing from other members of their co-culture. To confirm their distinctiveness with their co-cultural counterparts, some will participate in (or even possibly initiate) demeaning comments—racist, sexist, classist, heterosexist, and the like, jokes—and nonchalant banter that include poking fun at one's co-culture. The object of these remarks is usually a generalized co-cultural other who appears in the climax of a joke or comment featuring a well-known cultural stereotype. Nevertheless, in other instances, co-cultural group members may take part in comments directed at another person who is ostracized as a stereotypical representation of her or his co-cultural group.

> One day at the mall, I ran into a student who I knew from the dorms. Instead of being Americanized, she was the perfect image of the stereotypical subservient geisha girl. I didn't want my friends to think that all Asians were like that, so when she left I started mocking her.

Ridiculing self can take any number of direct or indirect forms. It can include derogatory comments initiated by another co-cultural group member, actively participating in telling offensive jokes, or merely laughing or nodding in agreement when dominant group members make insensitive remarks. In whatever form, the communicative practice of ridiculing self is engaged in as a means to appear like "one of the guys (dominant group)." The following comments are offered by an African American man reflecting on his college days:

> I am not proud of it, but I have sat and passively participated in some racist jokes. A couple of times little comments would be made about black stereotypes—you know, like eating watermelon and fried chicken—and I would laugh right along with them.

This man, like other co-cultural group members, generally interprets his inclusion in private dominant group conversations as evidence that he has been accepted as an ingroup member. In most cases, this occurs only after calculated measures to set oneself off as different from other co-cultural group members.

Using Liaisons

For African Americans who occupy positions in corporate America, McClenney (1987) asserts "your survival will depend on the help and assistance of good white men" (p. 19). So, besides intragroup networking described earlier, some co-cultural group members also find it necessary to identify specific dominant group members who can be counted on for support, guidance, and assistance during their interactions within dominant societal structures. Philipsen (1975) identifies this communicative practice as one often used by European Americans from a lower socioeconomic status, and Woods (1993) discusses the importance of gay men "choosing allies" (p. 118). Liaisons may include advisers, friends, colleagues, and empathic supervisors who were genuine, sensitive, honest, and open with their feelings. Nevertheless, it is not always easy to find dominant group members who are willing to act as liaisons and able to be trusted. One difficulty that co-cultural group members experience is in attempting to see through the guise of "political correctness" and hidden agendas of some dominant group members. This issue is apparent in the comments from one young African American male college administrator:

> I guess that I have found it very difficult to distinguish when they [in this case European American males] are sincere versus when they are trying to be politically correct—I struggle with that. They can talk the

> game, but I don't see them in action. I'm trying to trust them more, but I don't know where they are coming from.

Co-cultural group members report that it can take days or years to identify and collaborate with dominant group allies. At times, this process can be almost immediate whereas other relationships take years to develop to a point at which a certain level of trust is established. Only then can co-cultural group members begin to confide in their liaisons and take advantage of their privileged positioning.

Even when recognizing the benefits of liaisons, a few co-cultural group members experience a great deal of frustration with having to rely on the efforts of a liaison when they were fully competent to handle whatever situations arise. In a recent interview, one Korean American woman became physically agitated while telling of a problem situation with a European American female co-worker in which she had to rely on the influence of another European American female. A similar frustration was also apparent in a recollection from a Hispanic woman. After suffering a great deal of harassment and abuse from a (European American male) administrator,

> The only thing that worked was when we went to the affirmative action officer. But only after all that. You see, during the whole semester, I tried with him. First verbally, then in writing, then verbally again. Nothing worked. It was a disaster. Then only [through] force—through affirmative action and the administration—was it better the second semester.

Increasing Visibility

Some communicative behaviors adopted by co-cultural group members (e.g., emphasizing commonalities or mirroring) strive to diminish one's visibility when interacting with dominant group members. Nevertheless, some members of co-cultural groups apparently believe that their increased visibility as diverse people is just as important. "It seems that there is an attempt to neutralize everybody . . . and I don't like that," explained one African American woman. Different persons appeared to use a "strategy of presence" (McClenney, 1987, p. 28) to change how people view diversity in different settings. Instead of reinforcing the notion of "diversity as a detriment" and blending into the dominant culture, some co-cultural group members felt an increased need for visibility in attempts to counter existing negative attitudes toward diversity.

Specific tactics toward the goal of increased visibility include "occupying office space where others can see you" (African American man), "wearing obvious signs which symbolize my sexuality" (gay man), or "starting to attend events where my presence is felt" (Native American woman). For these co-cultural group members, the attempts to increase visibility generally are positive, yet lack the "IN YOUR FACE" intensity of more confrontational tactics (discussed later). These co-cultural practices are more subtle (e.g., assisting in the success of other co-cultural group members), yet unapologetic and distinct. As one African American woman explains, increasing one's visibility is one way to make your presence felt without necessarily evoking defensiveness in dominant group members:

> I like to make sure that I am "around" at different gatherings. I doubt my attendance at these events does anything to drastically change the opinions of others . . . [but] I do think that my mere presence changes the setting to some extent.

Confronting

Many of the co-cultural communicative practices that have been described thus far represent approaches that either sustain or (tactfully) contest the structures of dominant society. Other co-cultural group members, however, maintain that the only effective ways of getting their voices heard are through more aggressive confronting tactics. This type of communicative practice, described by one person as an "IN YOUR FACE" technique, ranges from malicious to belligerent behavior when interacting with dominant group members. For instance, one Asian American described a situation in a college class:

> He was the type of professor that didn't like questions during his lecture. But instead of following the stereotype that Asian women are subservient, and quietly do their work and get an A, I was always quick to raise my hand—*and my voice*—whenever I had a question. It clearly disrupted his train of thought, but I didn't care.

This woman also described several instances on and off her predominantly European American college campus in which she refused to be quiet, even to the point of being antagonistic with others who might question her abilities. "I've always been a little bit of a fighter," she went on to explain.

Although not all co-cultural group members feel comfortable using the practice of confronting, it does appear that some individual's personal styles encourage a more aggressive approach during co-cultural interaction. One Native American (Oneida) woman professes that she really doesn't "let anyone walk all over me—even if that means stepping on some toes." From some accounts it appears that co-cultural groups members become more fervent when interacting with dominant group members who seem most affected by their behaviors. A European American gay man described coming out and taking great pleasure in confronting heterosexuals with his homosexuality:

> I wore the dangling earrings and the flaming clothes . . . like walking down at the mall . . . *flaming* was not the word for me, I mean, I wanted everybody to know what I was like—[smacks hands together] *in your face* with it!

Confrontational tactics can take several forms: using coarse language, contentiously questioning dominant policies and practices, displaying aggressive nonverbalisms (like getting "in someone's face"), or giving dominant group members ultimatums. One Filipino American woman's comments, recounting police harassment at a gay rights conference (and especially her comments on "making more noise"), seem to capture the essence of confronting:

> I thought that we should sue. But the other people involved didn't want to. I guess that the new American way is to sue to get your issues out there. I know enough lawyers that like to make a big hoopla about everything [she laughs]. I think that when you make more noise, it gets more attention.

Gaining Advantage

One specific type of confrontation that different co-cultural group members practice involves exchanges by which they maliciously insert references to co-cultural oppression for the sole purpose of provoking a certain level of awkwardness and remorse among dominant group members. Steele (1990) refers to these types of manipulations as "power moves" and describes them as "little shows of power that try to freeze the 'enemy' in self-consciousness" (p. 4). In this regard, co-cultural group members strive to gain advantage (i.e., "to get the upper hand") when interacting with dominant group members:

> I get a little satisfaction by throwing my past [growing up in a housing project, on and off welfare] in their face. Everyone is generally pretty good about it . . . and very supportive and encouraging. But every now and then, I'll make certain comments that catch them off guard. Like once . . . when we were discussing childhood memories, everyone was talking about these "golden moments," so I said "the best thing that ever happened to us was when my father deserted us so that we could get more food stamps." I love to see their pitiful reactions!

Some co-cultural group members, as evident in the co-cultural communicative practice of educating others, find it important to expose institutional practices that are covertly discriminatory or subtle assertions of privilege that dominant group members take for granted. Nevertheless, persons who employ the practice of gaining advantage are not necessarily interested in enlightening dominant group members. Instead they are using this confrontational tactic to put others on the defensive and acquire some type of edge during interactions. Sometimes, co-cultural group members engage in this practice during discussions when they feel as if they "are on the losing side" and need a "surprise ace-in-the-hole." Others, as illustrated in the earlier example, use the tactic to keep their co-cultural diversity visible and acknowledged (often at the expense of others).

Bargaining

Beyond power moves, Steele (1990) describes how African Americans, as a co-cultural group, also "bargain" when interacting with European Americans. Bargaining is a communicative practice by which co-cultural group members strike an arrangement with dominant group members: They pledge to confirm dominant group members' innocence in societal oppression when they are accepted and allowed to participate in dominant-structured environments. According to Steele (1990), some African Americans have granted "white society its innocence in exchange for entry into the mainstream. . . . A bargainer says, *'I already believe you are innocent [good, fair-minded] and have faith that you will prove it'* " (pp. 10-11).

Other co-cultural group members bargain in similar ways to secure their participation in different settings. The rules are simple: "I promise not to make an issue of my co-cultural identity as long as you don't." To this end, attempts are made to separate co-cultural group members from their co-cultural identities while interacting within the confines of dominant societal structures. Spradlin (1995) reports that some lesbians participate in this process, which she calls "dissociating" (p. 4), to pass as heterosexual. The experiences of one Latino man in a predominantly European American office also indicate an "unspoken negotiation":

> I am the first and only Latino to be hired at my job. It's funny because all through the interview, my probation period, and last year, no one—except some of the black guys I hang around with—gave any indication that they have noticed that I'm not white. I mean they must have noticed . . . it's not like my last name is Smith or Jones. I guess that we have just struck an understanding where I don't make a big deal of it and neither do they.

Attacking

Earlier in this chapter, communicative practices such as developing positive face and censoring self were described as approaches that co-cultural group members engage in when communicating with dominant group members. Whereas these more "considerate" communicative practices are deemed appropriate by some, others reject them as inept and are not hesitant to use more antagonistic means to communicate with dominant group members. Sometimes, attacking involves the use of verbal aggressiveness as necessary to "get through to some folks."

Verbal aggressiveness can be defined as "inflicting psychological pain by attacking the other person's self-concept" (DeVito, 1995, p. 392) and includes verbal abuse and personal attacks. Co-cultural group members who use this practice when communicating with dominant group members are typically involved in one or more of the following behaviors: Insulting them by references to personal shortcomings, using offensive language, attacking their character, screaming and yelling, or using sarcasm. These behaviors, as a display of one's personal power, are considered apropos since they attempt to counter the institutional power of dominant group members. An African American female college student explains the reasoning behind using this aggressive co-cultural communicative practice:

> I used to try and be more friendly and cordial, but too often people walk all over you. So now, I let them know who they are dealing with. . . . Like this one time when __________ [the Director of Student Life] came up to me and started yelling about some damn room reservation, I told him "Fuck you! That's not my responsibility. Who do you think you're talking to, you little short bastard?" and walked away. I had to let him know that I wasn't playing.

When asked about how she could continue a working relationship with him after such a hostile altercation, she responded by saying "I don't need him. We got our [sorority] chapter and our own advisers—we going to take care of business regardless!" Clearly, in this case and others, co-cultural group members recognize that attacking may "burn some bridges," but are willing to deal with the consequences to secure the respect they deserve.

Sabotaging Others

Recent research indicates that a few co-cultural group members participate in what I have labeled "sabotage efforts" when involved with dominant group members. Sabotaging others represents a communicative practice in which co-cultural group members undermine dominant group members' ability to excel in environments that give them an inherent advantage over others. In other words, this tactic uses subversions to "make the playing fields a little more balanced." Such drastic measures are deemed necessary, especially in cases in which co-cultural differences are magnified and justification is given for special treatment. One young woman of European and Asian descent described using this practice in a public high school where "socioeconomic" distinctions were obvious:

> In our class, there were a group of students who thought that they were better than everyone else just because they had money. They would act like they were all that—walking around flaunting their

> designer clothes and all . . . and what made me really mad was that teachers would treat them better just because of it. So, a couple of times, my friends and me would steal their homework or get them in trouble with the teacher. It served them right.

In organizational settings, sabotaging others may include other behaviors that damage the overall effectiveness of the organization. For instance, co-cultural group members who are employees of companies run largely by dominant group members may "bad-mouth" the company to others to demonstrate their dissatisfaction. Other people may cut into the company's profits by stealing supplies, making long distance phone calls, or "borrowing" from petty cash. Most often these activities are deemed as "payback" for low wages or discriminatory practices as illustrated by the following narrative of an African American woman:

> My first job was as a cashier at ________ [a local grocery store]. The only reason that I got the job was because the NAACP had picketed his store because he [the owner] didn't have any blacks working there. So, he hired me and this other girl . . . he didn't like us and we hated the racist bastard. So, I made sure that whenever someone black came through my check-out lane that they got something for free. I would just bag it without ringing it up . . . most of the time I tried to give them free meat—or whatever was one of the most expensive items.

The co-cultural communicative practices described in this chapter represent a variety of ways in which nondominant group members communicate within dominant societal structures. Drawing from the experiences of co-cultural group members, an assortment of practices was identified: avoiding, averting controversy, maintaining interpersonal barriers, emphasizing commonalities, exemplifying strengths, mirroring, dissociating, dispelling stereotypes, manipulating stereotypes, embracing stereotypes, developing positive face, censoring self, extensive preparation, overcompensating, communicating self, educating others, intragroup networking, strategic distancing, ridiculing self, using liaisons, increasing visibility, confronting, gaining advantage, bargaining, attacking, and sabotaging others. Hardly is this inventory an all-encompassing list of how co-cultural group members communicate. As illustrated by the variety of approaches that people use to deal with cultural stereotypes, the multiplicity of communication tactics—and variations thereof—is limitless, constrained only by the limits of human ingenuity, resourcefulness, and determination for survival.

The intent of these explications was not to offer an exclusive list of co-cultural communicative practices but to familiarize the reader with the broad array of communication behaviors employed by those persons whose voices societal structures attempt to make inarticulate. How do co-cultural group members communicate in dominant society? From the assorted collection of practices described throughout this chapter, there is no one clear answer. Instead, it appears that although there is some ostensible consistency among how different co-cultural group members (people of color, women, gays and lesbians, etc.) communicate, it is also apparent that the ways in which they construe their experiences are not always similar. This concept is consistent with standpoint epistemology that is instrumental in recognizing structures that unite and differentiate co-cultural group experiences without necessarily essentializing them (Wood, 1992). Now that co-cultural communicative practices have been identified and explicated, Chapter 5 will explore the factors that influence the process by which co-cultural group members select which practices to employ when functioning within dominant societal structures. Such development is crucial to the clarification of co-cultural group experiences, as articulated by standpoint theorists (Wood, 1992):

> Researchers who operate from a standpoint posture begin by discovering the conditions that structure and establish limits on any particular person or group of people. Following that, researchers may ask how those conditions are understood and acted upon by various individuals. (p. 15)

Chapter 5

Clarifying a Co-cultural Communication Process

Identification and explication of the communication practices of co-cultural groups are valuable and important for understanding how persons, marginalized in dominant society, communicate with those who have direct access to institutional power. In essence, it represents a response to the underlying research question that guided the phenomenological inquiries that serve as the foundation for co-cultural theory: *What* is communication like for underrepresented group members? Although the great diversity of communicative practices described in Chapter 4 provides insight into this primary question, a description of co-cultural lived experiences, via a phenomenological hermeneutic spiral, provides additional understanding of the *hows* and *whys* of co-cultural communication. In this regard, each step of a hermeneutic analysis exemplifies a contextualizing reflection of lived experiences as they relate to the larger cultural context. Chapter 5 will provide a framework from which to conceptualize how co-cultural group members come to employ specific communicative practices. From the descriptions of those diverse co-researchers involved in the research projects on which this book is based, several assumptions can be made concerning this phenomenon.

First, co-cultural group members' communicative experiences can be seen as responses to dominant societal structures that label them outsiders. A clear acknowledgment of how power dynamics are manifested in everyday life appears to exist among co-cultural group members, who recognize that societal power is largely in the hands of European American males. Whereas African American men are specifically reminded to *"remember, it's always whites' ball"* (Orbe, 1994b) in their daily experiences, the lesson appears the same for other co-cultural group members who can attest that dominant group members (male, straight, upper income, etc.) largely "control the ball of life." The emerging "hyper-reflection" that captures *why* co-cultural group members employ an assortment of communicative practices is best compressed into one powerful phrase: *"because it is their world"* (see Orbe, in press).

The second key assumption regarding how co-cultural group members select specific communicative practices focuses on the transactional nature of the process. As explicated earlier, co-cultural communication is a dynamic ongoing process, not simply one decision made and followed by co-cultural group members. The selection of different communicative practices is the result of ongoing, constantly changing series of implementations, evaluations, and revisions. Decisions regarding co-cultural communication are not made in isolation by different co-cultural group members; they are simultaneously negotiated with dominant group members in several settings amidst a variety of circumstances.

Third, communicative practices are selected and employed for a variety of reasons. The grounds for using certain tactics during interactions may vary among co-cultural group members, but some rationale exists for these strategic choices. Although Madison (1993) is speaking specifically about African Americans, her comments illustrate the reasoning behind co-cultural "performance" when interacting with dominant group members:

> Contemporary experience demonstrates the roles black people perform for the benefit of whites—ranging from the obsequious Uncle Tom, the happy, harmless Negro, the dignified stoic, the lascivious whore or buck, the refined intellectual, the frightful street hood, and the uncompromising black militant—we see these types have traditionally been played out for a variety of purposes: to achieve certain ends or gains, for protection and security, or because performing them was the only effective or acceptable way to be seen and heard. (p. 223)

Clearly, employing certain communicative stances is seen as a strategic means to gain specific results. Cunningham (1992) concludes that a similar process of strategy selection exists for other co-cultural groups like lesbians and gays:

> Gay activists face a fundamental question familiar to feminists and civil rights leaders, among others. Do we play by the rules, court public sympathy, and push steadily but politely for recognition? Or do we make ourselves so unpleasant that yielding to our demands finally becomes easier than ignoring us? (p. 63)

A fourth assumption about the selection process is that each co-cultural group member has several strategic options from which to choose. Although some choices may be in clusters of similar practices (to be elaborated on toward the end of this chapter) or limited by other constraints, co-cultural group members typically use several tactics when interacting with dominant group members. This idea leads to the final assumption, that the process of selecting communicative practices is influenced by several interdependent factors. One of those factors may be job security, as indicated by the following narrative (Cebreco, quoted in Hunter, 1996) from a man who is disabled:

> When I first started working, I wouldn't say anything about my needs. . . . I felt like I was being pushy. . . . If I had to use the bathroom and they didn't have a handicapped-accessible rest room, I would just try to hold it. . . . I was afraid that if I asked for what I needed, I would lose my job. I've since found that you have to be assertive . . . to get what you need. (p. A4)

This abbreviated example serves as an effective depiction of how co-cultural group members come to adopt certain communication practices to achieve certain outcomes. In addition, it helps illustrate how co-cultural communication strategy selection is influenced by many interdependent factors that affect the choices made over time. The remaining sections of this chapter attempt to classify six universal factors—preferred outcome, field of experience, abilities, situational context, perceived costs and rewards, and communication approach—that influence the process by which co-cultural group members select communicative practices (see Figure 5.1).

Influential Factors

Preferred Outcome

One of the fundamental factors that influences the practices that co-cultural group members engage in is the preferred outcome for their interaction. Each person asks herself or himself the following question, "What communication behavior will lead to the effect that I desire?" To this end, co-cultural group members typically (consciously or unconsciously) give some thought as to how their communicative behavior affects their immediate and ultimate relationship with dominant group members. Although one's preferred outcome undoubtedly changes among—or even possibly in—different situations, three primary interactional outcomes emerged from the co-researchers' descriptions of lived experiences as options for persons outside the dominant structures in society: assimilation, accommodation, and separation.

Assimilation

Assimilation involves attempts to eliminate cultural differences, and the loss of any distinctive characteristics, to fit in with the dominant society. For some co-cultural group members, certain situations lend themselves to instances in which dominant group members falsely assume the identities of co-cultural group members. One African American female who works in management at a Fortune 500 company shares her experiences:

> That happens a lot at work; I work with the Florida markets, so before I go down there they think that they are talking to a white lady on the phone. . . . One lady even said, "You know that there aren't very many

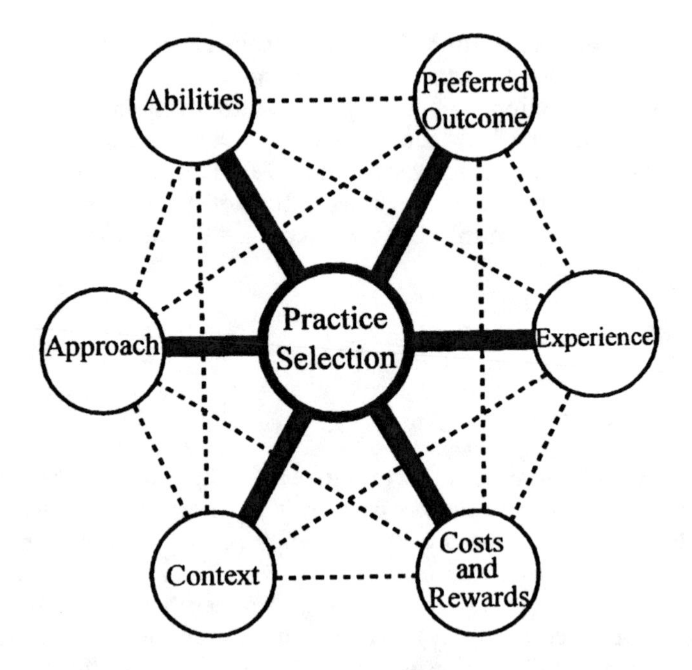

Figure 5.1. Influential Factors of Co-cultural Practice Selection

> of us WASPS left down here." So I was like, "Oh, okay." I didn't say anything, so I know that they think that I am white when they talk to me on the phone. They talk about me coming down there and getting a super tan and all this kind of stuff. That's fine with me as long as it doesn't affect my job performance.

Although some co-cultural group members who strive for assimilation into the dominant societal structures do so with little conscious effort, others make concerted efforts to "fit in," as reflected by the comments of an African American co-researcher:

> I think that for some of us there is a specific tendency to turn our radios down [when playing music associated with black culture], take up golf, and other things like that to say, "Oh, okay, I fit in. I'm like one of you guys now."

The reasoning behind the assimilation perspective is simple: To effectively participate in dominant society, you must conform to the structures of mainstream organizations. For co-cultural group members this translates into learning and using the communication structures of dominant society, while completely losing your own normal behavior or at least minimizing any differences to the point of marginal insignificance. Co-cultural group members are implicitly instructed that (borrowing from the old parental adage) "as long as you live in my house, you live by my rules." For nondominant group members (not unlike young children living with their parents), it is commonly understood that "my house" refers to the place of power that dominant group members own, operate, and reside in. Assimilation is the preferred outcome for those whose primary quest is to fit in with the expectations of dominant society. The following excerpt (Harvey Coleman, quoted in Wade, 1996) explains why this position is necessary:

> Top executive promotions aren't granted after a fun evening at the bowling alley or to men who wear earrings or to people who drive pickup trucks with gun racks. People who come from cultures where those things are normal have to decide if they want to stay where they are or move up. You can say that "I don't want to fit in." That's a choice but it probably means you are out of the game. (p. B14)

Accommodation

Whereas the co-cultural group members who operate within an assimilation perspective learn to "live by dominant societal rules," those functioning from an accommodation perspective insist that dominant structures "reinvent or, in the least, change the rules" so that they incorporate the life experiences of each co-cultural group. In this sense, the essence of accommodation is the development of appreciation, interdependence, and communicative skills to effectively work with persons from other cultures. Accommodation rejects the arguments for a great "melting pot" of cultures and instead promotes the collaborative strengths of multicultural society. In this regard, attempts to eliminate cultural differences or mute the voices associated with co-cultural groups are often resisted.

The experiences of one co-researcher vividly illustrate how preferred outcome can be a salient issue in contexts other than those involving corporate America. The comments below come from an African American lesbian who encountered some negative responses to showing affection for her lover when in the company of family members (family members maintained that her public displays of affection were inappropriate, not necessarily because it was same-sex affection):

> And I kept trying to give them the benefit of the doubt, but at the same time I knew that there was some underlying homophobia there. I almost blew if off, saying "well, they are just ignorant or whatever." . . . But then my aunt said something that made me think that she is purely homophobic. . . . She said that she "tolerates me because I'm family," and that she doesn't like the fact that I'm lesbian and would be tickled pink if I would come home with a man. Okay? I told her "Fuck you. I don't want to be tolerated by you. I don't have to be in your life."

As indicated by her comments above, this woman rejected the assimilation approach to diversity that promotes the invisibility—or at best tolerance—of co-cultural groups. In comparison, her attempt was toward an accommodation orientation, which focuses on the acceptance or inclusion of cultural differences as meaningful, valuable, and legitimate. Her final comment indicates that if accommodation is not an option for her family, separation is a distinct possibility.

Separation

Besides assimilation and accommodation, a third alternative for co-cultural group members is separation. The preferred outcome of separation rejects the notion of forming a common bond with dominant group members and other co-cultural groups. Instead, they seek to create and maintain separate-group identities outside or in dominant structures. As indicated by a 31-year-old African American male co-researcher, the choice of separation may result from a realization that it is futile to try to change or work within dominant structures:

> If you look at the plight of African Americans and other people of color in regards to the beginning of time in this country, an institutional legacy of racism has been ingrained and perpetuated through the years. It has been here so long that you or I are not going to change it.

Extending the metaphor included in the descriptions of assimilation and accommodation, separatists do not choose to "follow the rules" nor "work to change" them. Instead, they attempt to seclude themselves from dominant group members and "create their own rules." These efforts take several different forms apart or within mainstream structures but are circumscribed by the pervasiveness of the dominant culture in this society.

Instead of accepting the label of "extremist" often cast on co-cultural group members who adopt this approach, most maintain that they are simply trying to be realistic about intergroup relations, as illustrated by these comments (James Ezeilo, quoted in Hamilton, 1996) by a person of color:

> We're realists . . . the time for acceptance is long past. I think history taught us that there won't be true integration in the white corporate world or suburbs . . . so we build our own institutions and our own suburbs. (p. A4)

Although some co-cultural group members who adopt a separatist orientation assume a rigid stance, most practice some flexibility depending on situational circumstances. Others maintain different preferred outcomes at different stages in their lives. The descriptions of co-cultural group members gathered in the past 5 years revealed no clear standard among, or within, different groups. Instead, different co-cultural group members characterized their interaction with dominant group members as striving toward different outcomes depending on other influential factors.

Field of Experience

The interrelated nature of the six influential factors described in this chapter should become increasingly apparent as each factor is explicated. For instance, the field of experience (or sum of lived experiences) of each co-cultural group member directly affects his or her conceptualization of other factors and, consequently, his or her selection of co-cultural communicative practices. The incorporation of this factor into the analysis is significant since no two persons have identical fields of experience (standpoints).

The field of experience of each co-cultural group member directly affects his or her interaction with dominant group members. The influence of one's experiences is an important consideration in the constant, cyclical process of contemplating-choosing-evaluating co-cultural communicative practices. Through a lifelong series of experiences, co-cultural group members learn how to use a variety of tactics; they also come to realize the consequences of using certain practices in different situations. Through the multiplicity of incidents within their field of experience, co-cultural group members are engaged in constructing and subsequently deconstructing the perception of what constitutes "appropriate" and "effective" communication with dominant group members. The ways in which co-cultural group members process through this lifelong undertaking vary as much as their fields of experience themselves. One thing is certain: co-cultural group members (like their dominant group counterparts) are products of their life experiences. The comments from a Mexican American undergraduate attending a predominantly European American institution of higher learning in Dallas, Texas, illustrate this basic idea:

> My father's influence and general background has a lot to do with the way I act in public. He is 47 or 48, speaks broken English, and is a back-country Mexican, from the heart of Mexico, who is very conservative. We live in an all-Mexican neighborhood. It's kind of rough around here a little bit; we have gangs running around—I used to be in a gang. I got homies here and there. But I'm trying to clean up—not to say that I've done anything real bad, but I'm trying to do things right. But that doesn't mean forgetting who I am or where I came from.

Co-cultural group members describe several means of acquiring the knowledge and skills associated with different communicative practices while interacting with dominant group members. Some portray a natural inner propensity for certain co-cultural practices, like the African American man who shared that he "has a sixth sense when it comes to dealing with whites." Nevertheless, most persons describe three specific means within their field of experience that affect their current communicative practices.

Some co-cultural group members describe intragroup discussions in which specific guidance concerning dominant group members was shared. Many of these direct talks included discussions about the "lessons of life," a nuts-and-bolts approach to co-cultural existence, which were facilitated by family, friends, or acquaintances. The importance of this type of direct instruction is evident in the following narrative from an unwed mother of two biracial children:

> I remember the first time that I had to bring [my youngest daughter] into the clinic. I was real nervous and felt like the people there would look down on me for being on public aid. But [my significant other's] mother talked to me about it and told me how I should act.

For those who were not the recipients of frank, open exchanges concerning co-cultural communication, the second avenue, observation, was often adopted. Through observing how others communicate with dominant group members, some persons could decipher the intricate process of co-cultural communication. This means of tutelage, although not always as effective as direct instruction, was less uncertain than a trial-and-error process, described by some co-cultural group members as a third alternative. This tactic was viable since their field of experience lacked any tangible means to learn the "ins and outs" of communicating with dominant group members. The process of trial and error included trying new practices, learning from past mistakes, and constantly assuming risks. Without the direct support of other similar co-cultural group members, this process can be lengthy, ineffective, and frustrating.

Although co-cultural group members share some common experiences on the basis of their societal positioning, it is important to acknowledge that, depending on other cultural circumstances, each field of experience is unique. Through assortment of life experiences, co-cultural group members develop varying levels of group identity, need for social approval, and degrees of communication competence—all of which influence the process of selecting communicative practices.

Abilities

One factor that must be acknowledged in selecting co-cultural communicative practices is the person's relative ability to engage in different behavior. Most practices described in Chapter 4, given some thought, rehearsal, and motivation, appear to be accessible to all co-cultural group members. Nevertheless, the ability to use other co-cultural communicative practices may widely vary depending on specific personal characteristics and situational circumstances.

During the descriptions of lived experience, some members of co-cultural groups related that they do not have the "natural ability" to engage in certain practices that go against their personal style. For example, an African American woman characterized her nonassertive orientation as an insurmountable barrier to certain communicative practices, as confronting, attacking, and gaining advantage:

> Other people can do those things [more aggressive practices] well but that has never been something that I'm comfortable doing. . . . I am not much of a confrontational person, so I just like to get things done in different ways.

Other co-cultural group members might lack any reasonable opportunity to network with other co-cultural group members or have difficulty in identifying dominant group members that can be used as liaisons. Such was the case for two graduate students of color attending a large, predominantly European American institution of higher learning:

> I was the one person of color in all of my grad classes. . . . [There was this] one situation where I was in a class of where groups of three or so people divided up study questions that we had to do and exchanged them. And I am sitting there struggling to get all of mine done by myself, and you know . . . I felt like I didn't have anybody who I could relate to or work with.

> You are so busy all of the time that you never have a chance to get together [with other students of color] and say, "Yeah, this and that happened to me [too] and this is how it worked" . . . so you know you ain't crazy. It's never that come-together time.

A deeper examination of the assortment of co-cultural communicative practices reveals that one's ability to engage in each practice is something that should not be assumed. Given the circumstances inherent in different dominant structures and each person's perceived ability, co-cultural group members may not have the opportunity to behave in a certain way. The illustrations shared earlier provide insight into the nature of how this factor influences co-cultural decision making. Nevertheless, an extended treatment of one assimilation practice, mirroring, can serve as a more vivid illustration of the role that ability plays in the selection of co-cultural communicative practices.

Mirroring, which includes conscious attempts to clone the communicative behavior of dominant group members, is a practice that many co-cultural group members engage in, in their endeavor to "fit into mainstream society." Nevertheless, it is important to acknowledge that although co-cultural group members may strive to reproduce dominant group behavior, their ability to blend in is impacted by other personal characteristics. For instance, despite their attempts to become like dominant group members, some co-cultural groups—such as women, the physically or mentally challenged, or dark-skinned people of color—will inevitably not be able to "pass" as effectively as others (e.g., those from a lower socioeconomic background, or gays, or lesbians). This is not to say that these co-cultural group members are less likely to engage in mirroring; in fact, some of these persons may employ other practices such as strategic distancing and dissociating to further demonstrate their "likeness" with dominant group members. These activities, however, appear to be performed with clear awareness that their co-cultural identity is something that cannot be completely discarded. Reflections shared by one co-researcher clarify this notion:

> Well, I guess that I have to say that I've learned to feel most comfortable communicating as a black individual, and as a woman and a lesbian . . . second. I think that the first thing that stands out when someone sees me—the thing that means the most to them—is that I'm black. . . . There ain't no hiding it.

Another example of a co-cultural element that can be difficult or impossible to discard during interactions within dominant societal structures involves language use. To promote mirroring, some co-cultural group members master the ability to be "bidialectal," meaning that they learn how to communicate in the language of both dominant and co-cultural groups and employ the appropriate voice when the situation arises. Nevertheless, this ability is not something that is always inherent in the repertoire of each person's co-cultural communication competencies. Throughout the transcripts, some people of color described their inability to eliminate certain accents, phrases, speech mannerisms that immediately label them as an outsider in dominant structures. Other co-researchers, like those from a lower economic status or rural geographical area, described similar difficulties in trying to mirror the voices of dominant group members. The example of George's experiences (Woods, 1993) exemplifies how a co-cultural group member's ability level is affected by other factors (such as situational context). "I really demonstrate gayness in my voice," says George. "I wish I could have a different speech pattern and just be able to fade into the woodwork when I want to. But I don't." At least in the United States, George feels he has little choice but to come out in work settings. It's a different story, however, when he does business abroad. "By American standards I'm more effeminate than your average business man. But internationally that gets lost. You're suddenly an American, and there are so many other issues of difference that this pales in comparison." In part this explains George's decision to work for an airline that is headquartered in Europe. "My esteem is much better internationally," he says. "I probably speak German with a gay twang, but nobody seems to notice" (p. 89).

Situational Context

An important consideration in co-cultural communication is situational context, as illustrated in the case scenario of George. Without question, different practices are considered the most appropriate and effective depending on the specific situational circumstances. In this regard, a conscious attempt has been made throughout the descriptions of co-cultural communication theory to avoid commentary that would implicate certain practices as inherently more appropriate and/or effective than others. This presumption is consistent with the philosophy (described later) that one prototypical communication approach (e.g., assertiveness) does not exist for all situations. To suggest that some strategic decisions are "ideal" (and, in comparison, others less than ideal) would discredit the standpoints of diverse co-cultural group members. Clearly, no absolute model of co-cultural communication effectiveness is feasible given the multiple ways in which persons' experiences are situated.

Issues of situational context are central to the process of co-cultural communication. Co-cultural group members do not typically select one communicative practice, or cluster of practices, to use for all interactions with dominant group members. The complexity of communication processes does not allow such a simplistic "one-size-fits-all" approach. Instead, situational factors have a great impact on the calculation of how an assortment of variables or factors converges on the ultimate decision. One primary consideration related to this influential factor is the communication setting. Where is the interaction taking place? Generally, the conditions of a specific setting—work, home, school, public or social places—are an important point of attention in the selection of specific communicative practices. As one African American young man articulated, "I'm going to be black no matter what situation I'm in . . . but the ways in which that blackness is communicated depends on the specific situation." Without question, each of the influential factors discussed in this chapter (preferred outcome, communication approach, ability, field of experience, and perceived costs and rewards) affects and is affected by the situational context in which the co-cultural interaction occurs. For instance, in the following example, a woman's decision to engage in the communicative practice of manipulating stereotypes was directed toward accomplishing a specific goal (obtaining a reward); she makes it clear that this communicative practice is not appropriate for other situations:

> I have a car that has frequent mechanical problems. So I found that a co-worker's brother and all his nephews run a garage. And he [co-worker] was like "let me call my brother." So he called his brother and he's like "I'm going to send someone over, so you take care of her." . . . So, I'm using that "oh-please-I'm-helpless-take-care-of-me" thing. . . . I play that role for some things, like car mechanics, but for other things, in terms of "woman as victim" I never do.

The dynamics of power relations typically shift somewhat from situation to situation and this modification is reflected in which co-cultural communicative practices are employed. The narratives offered by various gay, lesbian, and bisexual co-researchers give voice to the ways in which persons negotiate their sexual orientation in different settings. Whereas some lesbigay people engage in clusters of communicative practices varying between work, family, and social settings, others maintain a consistent stance (out or closeted) regardless of the situation. One gay man reported that, although he "strives to be out wherever he goes," he admits to "hiding behind a cloak of assumed heterosexuality" when visiting family members. While describing his experiences during the recent funeral of a loved one, he explained that "[he] wanted to make it through with as little waves as possible." For gays and lesbians of color, situational context dramatically changes the saliency of issues related to co-cultural identity and consequently their employment of communicative practices.

> Being a person of color is more accepted than being a lesbian. . . . But really, you know as I think about it, I can't say that. It depends on what setting I'm in. . . . But what I'm thinking of is how I got it with my own family 2 weeks ago. My aunt had a fit because I kissed my girlfriend in front of her. . . . I may get that flak other places [but] that shit hurts because it involves people that I've known all my life.

Moreover, environmental changes may be apparent *within* a setting and directly influence the selection of communicative practices. For instance, students from underrepresented groups may experience different situational contexts all in a single day on campus (different classroom climates, cafeteria, student organization meeting, residence hall setting, library). Therefore, their primary co-cultural communicative practice in school may be altered depending on the specific context within the larger setting. The practices that are carried out can also be affected by the presence of others in that setting. The decision to opt for a distinct practice may be the direct result of the other parties in the interaction. (It is important to remember that co-cultural practices are employed interactionally with members of the dominant group.) Within the same setting, for example, co-cultural group members may take on assorted communicative practices when interacting with different dominant group members. As one Korean American woman described,

> It varies a lot. Some white male bosses are okay and others are not. Some treat you as a walking stereotype, while others don't seem to be phased. You have to determine what their deal is.

Clearly, co-cultural group members' communication approach (nonassertive, assertive, aggressive) and their preferred outcome (assimilation, accommodation, separation) may change depending on their perceptions of the person. Often, this includes a process of observation that lasts until specific conclusions can be drawn, as described by the following co-researcher:

> He [European American male administrator] simply would not listen to me at all. . . . I tried to talk with him . . . in formal settings or more formal ones . . . I saw him with men and he looked normal. I didn't have any idea about him but thought maybe he was a misogynist. . . . I don't know [because] my case is complicated because I am a woman and I am a Hispanic.

Moreover, the absence or presence of other co-cultural group members within a specific setting may influence which communicative practices are used. As depicted in the following, the decision to confront insensitive comments, for instance, might be influenced by the behavior of other co-cultural group members:

> For the longest time, I was the only woman at weekly meetings. And I was very conscious about my presence there. Whenever inappropriate comments about women were made I would bite my tongue and not respond. I guess that it was just the price for my participation. . . . This all changed when another woman joined the meetings. She was quick to challenge sexist comments. . . . [S]hortly after her arrival I found myself doing the same thing.

In this case scenario, the presence of another woman encouraged her to shift from the communicative practice of censoring self to one of communicating self or confronting. Other women, depending on the ways in which they negotiate the process of selecting communicative practices, may have opted for different alternatives (continued censoring self, educating others, or strategic distancing from the "radical feminist"). Much depends on how co-cultural group members perceive and react to the anticipated costs and rewards of their actions.

Perceived Costs and Rewards

As co-cultural group members engage in the ongoing process of selecting, employing, and evaluating the use of different communicative practices, one factor that is brought into consideration is the perceived costs and rewards associated with each practice. Depending on the specific situational context and preferred outcome, co-cultural group members will evaluate the anticipated costs and rewards of specific communicative practice differently; oftentimes this reflective process is governed by an individual's field of experience.

For instance, some co-cultural group members will select communicative practices whose benefits (communication effectiveness, social approval, or increased money or status) are given greater priority than the costs associated with those same practices (expended energy or time or criticism from other co-cultural group members). The following three narratives reflect instances when co-cultural group members clearly anticipated the costs and rewards before selecting a specific practice or cluster of communicative practices:

> I tend to be respectful and guarded with what I say, because I know that what you say can be a big reflection on your job . . . job security and stuff like that. I'm not always comfortable with it . . . but this involves my livelihood.
>
> (African American woman)

> And I'm like, "why are you telling me that [racist disclosure]? Why?" So, I look at him and I was really going to say something, but I'm a student and maybe I don't want to jump the gun. He's going to be teaching me for the next 2 years . . . so I decided to wait a little bit.
>
> (Mexican American man)

> The first time I was introduced to a gay couple I was shocked [because] I recognized both of them because every week they were always in the newspaper or the society pages with the most eligible women in the community. One worked as the top chief executive for a huge brokerage home and the other was chief operating officer at a large insurance agency. . . . They talked about owning two homes . . . keeping different bedrooms with one's clothes in one closet and the other's belongings in the other bedroom, even down to cologne. . . . They always spent the holidays apart, attended social events apart, and never appeared in public together. . . . They knew that this [information concerning their sexual orientation] could have ended both of their careers. This is a lesson we all learn.
>
> (European American gay man)

It is important to recognize that weighing the costs and rewards of each situation often varies depending on the field of experience of the specific co-cultural group member. For instance, one of the previous narrators appeared to give priority to certain rewards (e.g., career or academic success), whereas other co-researchers articulated that the costs (e.g., stress, burnout, or losing one's self-respect) associated with these things were not worth the effort to obtain them. Moreover, the ways in which co-cultural group members process this information are not always clear; oftentimes deliberations involve a multitude of perceptions slanted by the standpoint of co-cultural group members. Given the pervasiveness of dominant ideologies, some perceive their choices as severely limited and constrained by their lack of power. The level of satisfaction from selecting certain communicative practices, and the consequences of each activity, depends largely on the expectations of co-cultural group members—something that is generally shaped from within their field of experience. An important consideration is that, although this decision-making process assumes that co-cultural group members can accurately anticipate the consequences of a variety of interactions, such is not always the case.

The strategic decisions that co-cultural group members make regarding their communication with dominant group members involve varying awareness levels of available alternatives and a predictive understanding of consequences associated with different practices. Each co-cultural communicative practice has some rewards and costs associated with it (albeit sometimes difficult to calculate). For instance, co-cultural group members may engage in the practice of extensive preparation and overcompensation in their attempts to prove their worth in dominant group settings (reward). Nevertheless, such efforts must brave conditions that are prone to stress, burnout, and animosity from both co-cultural and dominant group members (costs). The same is true for other practices, such as communicating self, that are often regarded as "seemingly appropriate" and potentially full of positive effects. Yet self-assured communicators must also contend with dominant group members who view them as "not knowing their place." The idea that each co-cultural communicative practice has potential rewards and costs is treated in more detail in subsequent sections. Given the multifarious operations of considering the pros and cons of communication practices, this process is complex, multidimensional, and constantly in flux. Some co-cultural group members, for instance, are not only concerned about how their communicative practices affect their futures. As articulated by an African American male co-researcher, many are also cognizant of how their actions also impact other co-cultural group members.

> Typically I'm gonna do what I need to do . . . [but] I also see the bigger picture. If I feel that I may be the first, or one of the very few black men that they have come in contact with, then yes, that might affect the way that I communicate with them. I know that my actions affect how they see all black men.

Communication Approach

The final factor recognized as influential in the process by which co-cultural group members select, employ, and evaluate communicative practices is communication approach. For the purposes of co-cultural theory, communication approach is used to connote practices that fall along the continuum of nonassertive, assertive, or aggressive behavior. Nonassertive communicative practices include behavior by which individuals are *seemingly* inhibited and nonconfrontational while putting the needs of others before their own. Some co-researchers attributed their soft-spoken style as inherent to their specific culture (e.g., first-generation Asian American women); however, other co-cultural group members explained that their nonassertive approaches were more of a strategic decision in certain situations. One female co-researcher who works in a Fortune 500 company describes how this process works with her male supervisors:

> I know what all of the research says about women using less powerful speech—like tag questions, for example. But don't be fooled! Some of us women purposely use these things to get our points across. . . . We know that some men won't listen to women who come off as too confident.

This strategic approach was also reflected by a Native African American man who noticed that his supervisors (mostly European American women) became threatened by his creativity and energy:

> I find myself even having to approach them differently, with a softer tone. I have to go in there and really make it seem like. . . . "What you're saying is true, I understand and I agree with you. And that is great and

> it is fine, but what if we just turned this a little bit this way—using your idea, your concepts, let's turn it a little this way." I get my point across and they say "Oh, yeah, that will work!"

Aggressive communicative practices would describe those activities *perceived* as hurtfully expressive, self-promoting, and assuming control over the choices of others. Whereas certain co-cultural communicative practices assume a nonassertive stance, others such as confronting, attacking, or sabotaging others clearly take on a more aggressive stance. Often, a more aggressive approach is used by co-cultural group members when previous (nonassertive or assertive) attempts were unsuccessful. Such is the case with one African American male high school student who spoke at great length about his attempts to improve the treatment of minorities in his high school:

> At one point it got real ugly . . . I mean calling names, threatening lawsuits, personal attacks—you wouldn't believe it. But that was the first time that they seen that I really meant business about being pro-black. They realized at that point that I wasn't looking to just fit in and get my degree. . . . I was saying respect the black students at this school. . . . And a whole lot of white students finally said, "He's nothing to play with."

Representing a balance between the borders of nonassertiveness and aggressiveness, assertive communicative practices encompass self-enhancing, expressive behavior that takes into account both self and others' needs. In other words, co-cultural group members who strive for an accommodating voice do so with a clear attempt to promote their own rights, needs, and desires without violating the rights of others (both dominant group members and other co-cultural group members). Equally important to note, certain assertive practices when employed by co-cultural group members may be perceived as aggressive moves by dominant group members. Such was the case with a female undergraduate science major:

> I found that in small groups men tend to have no faith in my abilities or my suggestions. I hate it when I know what I am talking about and someone tries to shrug me off for no reason. So I try to say my piece without stepping on any toes but sometimes it just comes across as "we are going to do it this way, no ifs and ands about it."

Some co-cultural group members describe their interaction with dominant group members as guided by a "natural" tendency toward a specific approach (for example, nonassertive: "It's not my style to yell, so I do things more quietly"). Others possess a more balanced proficiency to be nonassertive, assertive, or aggressive and strategically select which approach is most effective (for example, assertive: "She appreciates an open, honest approach to decision making," or aggressive: "Yelling and screaming are the only things that work with him") in that specific situation.

As articulated earlier, a central premise for co-cultural theory involves the recognition of diverse standpoints as equally valid. An earlier discussion of preferred outcomes made it clear that no one orientation (assimilation, accommodation, or separation) was inherently "correct"; an individual's preference for one outcome over the other is navigated through a complex process of interrelated factors. In similar fashion, co-cultural theory functions with the belief that one communication approach is not more appropriate or ideal than others. Each co-cultural practice, as it reflects a general nonassertive, assertive, or aggressive communication approach, can be effective and/or appropriate depending on how the specific co-cultural group member perceives the situation. Given the following comments, it is evident that no clear preference for one communication approach over the other exists among co-cultural group members.

> Some will fight differently. Some gay men say, "Why stand up and tell people that you are gay? Just sit down and be quiet." Some people feel that way; I don't. We are all individuals, we are all different.
>
> (European American gay youth)

> I told them [European Americans who were intimidated by my comments] that I don't mean to make people scared of me, that is far from what I'm trying to do. I want people to respect me. I had problems with some blacks too; they felt that I was too strong . . . too political with my words.
>
> (African American male student)

Thematic Revelations via the Hermeneutic Spiral

Phenomenological inquiry, according to Warnick (1979), "cannot be an external, after-the-fact analysis but emerges from a processual, in vivo study" (p. 261) of the descriptions of lived experiences. The conceptualization of co-cultural communication theory reflects the ideals articulated by Warnick in that the various communicative factors for selecting those practices in this chapter emerged from the co-researchers' narratives. These scholarly insights, conceived from a "hyper-reflective" reviewing of diverse lived experiences, were generated through the continuing hermeneutic spiral inherent in phenomenology.

In her 1979 article, Warnick proposes that scholars avoid the polarization of structuralism and phenomenology and examine how *parole* (individual act of communication) and *langue* (the background against which *parole* is performed) interrelate in our everyday communication. This ontological directive, also consistent with Merleau-Ponty's (1964) work, inherently guides the conceptualization of co-cultural communication theory. The framework presented in this book provides insight into intricate interlocking factors that guide the process (*langue*) by which co-cultural group members select various co-cultural communication practices (*parole*).

The discussion of six interrelated factors—preferred outcome, field of experience, abilities, situational context, perceived costs and rewards, and communication approach—and the ways in which they inform the process of selecting co-cultural communicative practices represents a hermeneutic step beyond the initial thematizations described in Chapter 4. In this regard, the emergence of these six factors constitutes a contextualizing reflection by which phenomenological inquiry gains access to the larger cultural context through the lived experiences of its co-researchers. The hermeneutic spiral, in this context, generates insight into the process of co-cultural communication as it is inside a discursive space of "muted" and dominant group interactions:

> Situated within a particular *field of experience* that governs their perceptions of the *costs and rewards* associated with, as well as their *ability* to engage in, various communication practices, co-cultural group members will adopt communication orientations—based on their *preferred outcomes* and *communication approaches*—to fit the circumstances of a specific *situation*.

The interrelatedness of these six factors became clear during the descriptions provided earlier in this chapter; the interlocking nature of factors made it difficult (essentially impossible) to discuss one factor without addressing its relationship with other factors. For the sake of clarity in initially describing these elements, however, a conscious attempt was made to bracket these associations. Once these elements were described in some detail the interrelatedness of the factors could be revealed as multidimensional structures for co-cultural experiences of "existential reality" (Hyde & Smith, 1979, p. 347). Hence, the overriding characterization of the co-cultural communication process just articulated is effective in providing insight into issues that guide the selection of specific communicative practices. These descriptions notwithstanding, additional infrastructures among these factors continued to emerge as these thematic insights were merged (with earlier concepts) into the self-reflexive hermeneutic spiral. These emerging associations add further insight into the process by which co-cultural group members communicate with dominant group members.

The Emergence of Communication Orientations

The description of co-cultural communication shared above contained the term *communication orientation,* a concept referring to a specific stance that co-cultural group members assumed during their interactions in dominant societal structures. The notion of a co-cultural communication orientation emerged from the descriptions of lived experience to depict how a communicative stance is assumed through the conscious and unconscious processes of assessing-selecting-implementing-and-evaluating communication behavior. As explicated earlier, this process is guided by six interrelated factors. The concept of communication orientation focuses on how three of these factors—communication approach, preferred outcome, and perceived costs and rewards—converge to formulate nine different communicative stances inherent in co-cultural communication. With respect to explicating these communication orientations, it is important to recognize that these positions are within a distinctive field of experience for each co-cultural group member and within a specific situational context, both of which directly influence the ability to engage in certain practices. In other words, the adoption of a specific communication orientation, although it reflects the consideration of three specific factors (communication approach, preferred outcome, and perceived costs and rewards), occurs with a clear recognition of the ways in which this decision is affected by the other three factors (field of experience, abilities, and situational context).

During the three-step process of pheomenological inquiry—description, reduction, and interpretation—noticeable similarities and differences were apparent among the 26 communicative practices described in Chapter 4. Clusters of certain types of practices, for example, appeared strikingly similar in regard to their communication approach; others materialized as prominently different. A corresponding differentiation also emerged of the ways in which different types of communicative practices were used to achieve specific preferred outcomes. The decision to employ clusters of comparable practices, meaning those that share a common preferred outcome and communication approach, occurs with a clear discernment of the costs and rewards associated with each decision.

Drawing from descriptions explained earlier in this chapter, communicative practices could be distinguished as generally nonassertive, assertive, or aggressive in nature. Distinctions between which practices constitute nonassertive, assertive, or aggressive behavior (especially those that could be interpreted in one of two ways) were made through a reexamination of how co-cultural group members described their actions. Similarly, co-cultural communicative practices can be clustered along the lines of how they promote a general outcome (assimilation, accommodation, or separation). Without question, practices can be innovatively employed via several communication approaches to achieve a variety of preferred outcomes. Nevertheless, the conceptualization of practices presented in Figure 5.2 represents the emergence of nine communication orientations adopted during their interactions within dominant societal structures *from the standpoint of co-cultural group members.* The remaining portion of the chapter will describe the essence of each communication orientation.

Nonassertive Assimilation

Three basic orientations exist (depending on the particular preferred outcome for that situational context) when co-cultural group members use a nonassertive approach when functioning in dominant society. One option is a nonassertive assimilation orientation. As illustrated in Figure 5.2 in the upper right-hand cell, a nonasser-

	Separation	Accommodation	**Assimilation**
Nonassertive	Avoiding Maintaining interpersonal barriers	Increasing visibility Dispelling stereotypes	Emphasizing commonalities Developing positive face Censoring self Averting controversy
Assertive	Communicating self Intragroup network-ing Exemplifying strengths Embracing stereotypes	Communicating self Intragroup networking Using liaisons Educating others	Extensive preparation Overcompensating Manipulating stereotypes Bargaining
Aggressive	Attacking Sabotaging others	Confronting Gaining advantage	Dissociating Mirroring Strategic distancing Ridiculing self

Figure 5.2. Co-cultural Communication Orientations

tive assimilation orientation typically involves co-cultural communicative practices such as emphasizing commonalities, developing positive face, censoring self, and averting controversy, to blend unobtrusively into dominant society. These efforts are employed in a seemingly, yet sometimes strategically, inhibited stance that tries to avoid conflict with dominant group members.

Like each communication orientation, nonassertive assimilation involves potential benefits and costs for co-cultural group members who assume this communicative stance. Nonassertive assimilation may be advantageous for co-cultural group members who seek to be regarded as persons whose goal is to focus on task production and/or social standing. In this regard, a nonassertive assimilation orientation to co-cultural communication may enhance a person's ability to participate within the confines of dominant structures. Nevertheless, this communicative stance also produces several potential costs. Through this positioning, co-cultural group members may endure negative effects on their self-concepts. In addition, engaging in the communicative practices associated with this orientation promotes an unhealthy communication climate that inherently reinforces the dominant group's institutional and social power.

Assertive Assimilation

Similar to their nonassertive counterparts, those with assertive assimilation orientations strive to downplay co-cultural differences and promote a convergence into existing structures within dominant society. Instead of doing so in a presumably passive voice, however, this primary communication orientation employs a more assertive communication approach. In this regard, an assertive assimilation orientation enlists communicative practices that do not necessarily provide given privileges to either self or others' needs.

Those co-cultural group members who adopt this orientation employ communicative practices such as extensive preparation, overcompensating, manipulating stereotypes, and bargaining (see middle right cell in Figure 5.2). Bargaining, for instance, described in the previous chapter, relates to instances when co-cultural and dominant group members negotiate an arrangement by which neither party will make an issue of co-cultural differences. The preferred outcome (reward) is to fit into dominant structures; co-cultural group members can focus on being productive "team players" while demonstrating their ability to achieve a certain degree of "success" in life.

Nevertheless, the means by which this preferred outcome is achieved involves some costs for both participants. The commitment toward personal, social, and/or organizational success, coupled with the additional efforts necessary to suppress one's co-cultural identity to blend into dominant societal structures, is often accompanied by a significant amount of exertion, stress, and burnout. In addition, certain communicative practices, such as manipulating stereotypes and overcompensating, may reinforce co-cultural stereotypes and power differences associated with an "us-them" mentality. In any case, those co-cultural group members assuming an assertive assimilation stance typically find it difficult to persevere with this orientation; in the end, the productivity of both co-cultural and dominant group members may suffer.

Aggressive Assimilation

Whereas some co-cultural group members assume a nonassertive or assertive approach to becoming an integral part of dominant structures, others take a more aggressive communication approach. As compared to nonassertive or assertive assimilation orientations, the co-cultural communicative practices that these persons employ are generally perceived as more self-promoting and/or hurtfully expressive. In this regard, a person who uses an aggressive assimilation orientation takes a determined, sometimes belligerent, stance in his or her efforts to be seen as one of the dominant group. Co-cultural group members who use this primary communication orientation, which includes dissociating, mirroring, or strategic distancing (lower right cell in Figure 5.2), place great importance on fitting in—to the extent that others' rights and beliefs are viewed as less important in comparison. The tendency to engage in self-ridicule (i.e., derogatory banter or jokes concerning co-cultural groups) illustrates the magnitude to which some co-cultural group members will go to be perceived as dominant group members.

The benefits associated with an aggressive assimilation orientation revolve around the co-cultural group member's ability to fit into dominant structures and be regarded as an individual (avoiding the label of "typical" co-cultural group member). Nevertheless, these benefits do not occur without the potential to incur several costs.

Beyond expending significant amounts of time and energy on the communicative practices associated with aggressive assimilation, these efforts may also solicit negative reactions from other co-cultural group members. Aggressive assimilationists find themselves repeatedly negotiating their position in dominant societal structures while being isolated from other co-cultural group members who often label them as "self-hating sellouts."

Nonassertive Accommodation

Sometimes, co-cultural group members strive to blend in with dominant group members. In other situations, the preferred outcome is to have their co-cultural identity recognized and appreciated. Inherent in an accommodation perspective is a desire to change dominant structures to include reflections of co-cultural group experiences. Those persons using the primary communication orientation of nonassertive accommodation attempt to achieve this preferred outcome in a seemingly constrained and nonconfrontational manner.

As displayed in Figure 5.2 (upper middle cell), nonassertive accommodationists employ co-cultural communicative practices such as increasing visibility and dispelling stereotypes when functioning in dominant societal structures. Although some instances of these strategic efforts may be considered more assertive than nonassertive, most co-cultural group members describe using both communicative practices to "delicately" challenge the status quo of dominant group structures. This strategic interaction was initiated, through an inhibited voice, so that dominant group members would not react with defensiveness or circumspection. In this regard, a nonassertive accommodation orientation allowed co-cultural group members to influence in-group decision-making processes while simultaneously demonstrating their commitment to the larger group goals.

Although the potential benefits of this communication orientation are readily apparent for both co-cultural and dominant group members, several potential costs also exist. Nonassertive accommodationists often are criticized by other co-cultural group members (especially those who adopt the five orientations described later) as too passive and unwilling to take risks in challenging dominant societal structures. Another detriment associated with this orientation involves the reality that, whereas nonassertive accommodationists can subtly influence certain issues, this communicative stance if used consistently is unable to promote major change.

Assertive Accommodation

Some co-cultural group members, like those using a nonassertive assimilation orientation, are often overly concerned with dominant group reactions. For others, regard for dominant group rights is not given preference over their own needs as co-cultural group members. Instead, efforts aimed to create a cooperative balance between consideration for both co-cultural and dominant group members guide their behavior. These persons often find themselves using an assertive accommodation orientation when interacting in dominant societal structures.

Several co-cultural communicative practices appear to promote the goal of accommodation through an assertive voice (center box in Figure 5.2). Through such practices as communicating self, intragroup networking, using liaisons, and educating others, assertive accommodationists could work with others (co-cultural and dominant group members) to change existing dominant structures. Besides promoting intergroup interdependence, co-cultural group members who adopt an assertive accommodation stance can employ a wide variety of valuable resources in their quest to promote significant change in the structures that attempt to oppress co-cultural group experiences. Potential costs associated with this communication orientation involve being prone to stress and burnout as well as criticisms from others (e.g., co-cultural group members who adopt the three different separation orientations) who regard their efforts to "work with, instead of against" dominant group members as misled. Moreover, persons who assume an assertive accommodation stance may be confronted with resistance and defensiveness by dominant group members who perceive their attempts to maintain an assertive voice as aggressive.

Aggressive Accommodation

The focus of an aggressive accommodation orientation is on becoming a part of dominant structures and then working from within to promote significant change despite personal costs. At times these efforts may be perceived as self-promoting, confrontational, or unnecessarily intense, but co-cultural group members who adopt this primary communication orientation are not overly concerned with dominant group perceptions. Their fundamental goal is to change dominant structures.

Aggressive accommodationists, although fighting for societal change, must also cultivate their genuine desire to work with, and not necessarily against, dominant group members. Using practices such as confronting and gaining advantage, illustrated in the lower middle cell in Figure 5.2, co-cultural group members may be able to strike such a balance. But to avoid dominant group perceptions of their behavior as more separatist in nature, co-cultural group members who employ an aggressive accommodation orientation to intergroup relations may periodically use practices of the assertive accommodation orientation. In this regard, they can reap the benefits of such a position (along with the positive perceptions of their honesty, persistence, and commitment to promoting societal change) while eluding several potentially harmful effects. Co-cultural group members who consistently embrace an aggressive accommodation orientation stand the risk of being labeled as "overly sensitive," a "radical," or "someone constantly crying wolf." These persons also risk surviving in a dominant societal structure, isolated from both dominant and co-cultural group members who do not want to be associated with some of their more aggressive practices. This, in turn, makes their ability to promote major institutional change more difficult.

Nonassertive Separation

With regard to co-cultural differences, our society is one that is typically segregated regarding where we live, work, learn, pray, and play. Ethnic and class divisions are apparent to most Americans. Nevertheless, after some introspection, segregation among other co-cultural groups, like women, men, gays, lesbians, or bisexuals, can also be seen to occur at varying levels. Some co-cultural group members view separation as a "naturally occurring" reality; others use subtle communicative practices to maintain a separatist stance during co-cultural group interactions.

As represented in the upper left-hand cell in Figure 5.2, co-cultural communicative practices such as avoiding and maintaining interpersonal barriers are often employed to further encourage co-cultural separation. For those co-cultural group members assuming this primary communication orientation, physical avoidance is implemented whenever possible. Nevertheless, when some interaction with dominant group members is unavoidable co-cultural group members find themselves fulfilling existing expectations placed on them by dominant society. In other words, co-cultural group members unconsciously participate in efforts to reinforce co-cultural separation, an ideology grounded in the basic notion that certain groups should not occupy spaces reserved for dominant group members. Whereas this communication orientation can encourage intragroup unity, self-determination, and independence (potential benefits), it also hinders co-cultural group members by tapping into their valuable resources and advocating societal change (potential costs).

Assertive Separation

Compared to a nonassertive separation orientation, an assertive separation stance involves more self-assuredness in co-cultural attempts to create productive in-group structures exclusive of dominant group members. Co-cultural group members who adopt a nonassertive separation orientation simply, albeit somewhat passively, maintain existing separation between groups. In comparison, more assertive co-cultural group members actively counter hegemonic messages that signify that "natural separation" is a product of cultural superiority or inferiority differences. In this regard, an assertive separation orientation results in a conscious choice to maintain societal spaces between dominant and co-cultural group members. To this end, an assertive separation orientation entails co-cultural communicative practices such as exemplifying strengths and embracing stereotypes.

From the standpoint of co-cultural group members, assertive practices that could be effectively used toward the preferred outcome of accommodation could also be equally productive in separatist endeavors (left middle cell in Figure 5.2). For instance, communicating self and intragroup networking appear to be co-cultural communicative practices that both assertive accommodationists and separatists employ with equal success. The consequences of these co-cultural practices, in relation to the achievement of a preferred outcome, are contingent on other influential factors such as situational context and field of experience. One of the benefits of an assertive separation orientation, like its nonassertive counterpart, is that it promotes co-cultural unity and self-determination. In addition, this communication orientation also can enhance the self-concepts of co-cultural group members through increased visibility of positive co-cultural group role models.

Nevertheless, the efforts of co-cultural group members who assume an assertive separation orientation to intergroup relations must be implemented without access to most of the resources controlled by dominant group members. For their progroup rhetoric (exemplifying strengths), assertive separatists are often designated as an "antidominant group" (as opposed to simply pro–co-cultural group) by dominant group members. This outsider position reduces the ability of co-cultural group members to influence decisions made outside their specific communities, including many decisions that directly or indirectly affect their livelihood.

Aggressive Separation

Sometimes perceived by dominant and co-cultural group members as radically iconoclastic, an aggressive separation stance is a primary communication orientation that co-cultural group members employ when co-cultural segregation is a top priority. In other words, separation is sought through "whatever means necessary." These persons are likely to strongly criticize other co-cultural group members who habitually adopt an assimilation or accommodation orientation since their efforts are viewed as ill guided, inconsequential, and potentially destructive.

As depicted in the lower left cell in Figure 5.2, a person with an aggressive separation orientation to co-cultural interaction seeks to exert his or her personal power through co-cultural communicative practices such as attacking and sabotaging others. As described in Chapter 4, these two practices involve personal attacks on dominant group members' characters and livelihoods. Whereas the levels of personal and group power used by co-cultural group members who adopt an aggressive separation orientation do not match the societal power bases of dominant group members, they do enable some co-cultural group members to confront the pervasiveness of dominant structures on a smaller level. In this regard, these individuals can demonstrate the intragroup power of co-cultural solidarity while maintaining a strong voice in confronting the "evils" of dominant society. Nevertheless, it is exactly the strength and intensity of these voices that often make them unlikely to be muted and, consequently, largely unnoticed within dominant societal structures. Co-cultural group members who assume an aggressive separation communication orientation also risk displays of power (e.g., legal, political, or institutional retaliation for aggressive tactics) by dominant group members who retaliate against co-cultural aggressive practices.

Following the descriptions of the general characteristics of each communication orientation, it is important to recognize several points to effectively use this framework to fully understand the communicative experiences of co-cultural group members. First, various co-cultural communicative practices beyond those included in Figure 5.2 are possible within the nine primary communication orientations identified. The practices described are offered to illustrate how clusters of similar co-cultural communicative practices comprise various orientations toward intergroup relations.

A second point to note is how the nine co-cultural communication orientations are manifested within the transactional process inherent in co-cultural group members' selection of specific communicative practices. This process is one that involves a constant progression of self-assessment, innovation, and modification and is simultaneously negotiated with the co-cultural and dominant group members involved in the interactions. In this regard, the communication orientations that emerge from clusters of co-cultural practices are given meaning through the episodic interactions in dominant societal structures. Some co-cultural group members may have an exemplary communication orientation that is assumed consistently across situational contexts with little attention to other factors. Yet still other co-cultural group members find themselves assuming a variety of orientations (albeit sometimes in small variations) depending on the other influential factors identified earlier in this chapter.

This is an important consideration because it demonstrates how the diverse standpoints (*field of experience*) of co-cultural group members affect the process of adopting different communication orientations during the interactions with dominant group members. Although this should be obvious when considering distinct co-cultural groups such as people of color, gays, lesbians, or bisexuals, intragroup diversity should also be recognized when examining one specific co-cultural group. In other words, the variance of communication orientations within one group (e.g., Asian Americans) is most likely just as great as the divergence among co-cultural groups. The *ability* to employ certain practices, and in turn specific co-cultural orientations, will vary depending on the *situational context* and the *perceived costs and rewards* associated with each strategy. Whereas the descriptions in this chapter are not intended to be all-inclusive or definitive, they do suggest the complexity of information inherent in co-cultural group members' communicative decisions. Depending on their field of experience—especially past incidents with dominant group members—co-cultural group members may perceive the costs and rewards associated with each orientation in very different ways. In fact, some will perceive the same consequence (for instance, being perceived as "a radical") as a benefit or cost depending on their convictions and *field of experience.*

A central issue to the selection of co-cultural practices and, in turn, adoption of communication orientation, is *situational context.* Through their unique *fields of experience,* co-cultural group members differentiate the intergroup dynamics existing in different physical settings. For instance, the descriptions of lived experiences provided by the co-researchers involved in the four research projects summarized in this book indicated that the perceived costs and rewards akin to one communication orientation may change drastically when evaluated in a social versus professional setting. Recognizing this divergence, co-cultural group members will make strategic decisions accordingly.

Even within one specific context, members of different co-cultures may find that they must also employ a conglomeration of communication orientations to maintain a certain level of effectiveness. For instance, if preferred outcome is the salient issue for co-cultural group members in the workplace, then they may employ communicative practices listed across the nonassertive, assertive, and aggressive cells of Figure 5.2. Their ultimate effectiveness at achieving a preferred outcome may be greatly affected by their abilities to decipher which communication approach is most likely to elicit the most favorable response. If the preferred outcome is accommodation, for example, a co-cultural group member may recognize that using assertive practices (intragroup networking or educating others) are effective when interacting with certain dominant group members but ineffective with others. In these instances, more aggressive communicative practices (e.g., confronting) are necessary to promote change within the dominant structures. Through a constant process of selecting, implementing, and evaluating communicative practices, some co-cultural group members may recognize that certain orientations are not cultivating desired results as planned and shift to another communication orientation within a specific interaction.

In summary, this chapter identified and explicated six interdependent factors that influence the process by which co-cultural groups select various communicative practices. In addition, nine communication orientations as described through the lived experiences of diverse co-cultural group members were briefly introduced and explained. Through the reflective lens of a hermeneutic spiral, the essence of co-cultural communication was captured:

> Situated within a particular *field of experience* that governs their perceptions of the *costs and rewards* associated with, as well as their *ability* to engage in, various communicative practices, co-cultural group members will adopt communication orientations—based on their *preferred outcomes* and *communication approaches*—to fit the circumstances of a specific *situation.*

The final chapter of this book will reflect on the conceptualization of co-cultural communication theory and explore the strengths, limitations, and implications of the framework as it relates to existing communication theory. Moreover, Chapter 6 will offer a discussion of the implications for future research in the area of co-cultural communication.

Chapter 6

Limitations, Extensions, and Future Directions

The development of co-cultural theory is an attempt "to bring to light the clandestine forms taken by the dispersed, tactical, and [makeshift] creativity of groups or individuals" (de Certeau, 1984, p. xvii) living in a society in which they are not part of the dominant culture. Often made invisible by traditional research designs that strongly reflect a dominant group perspective, these forms of communication inventiveness represent a valuable source of insight for the field of communication. The nine primary communication orientations identified here, as well as the various practices commonly associated with each orientation, are valuable in gaining insight into the intricacies of intercultural communication—especially those encounters between a variety of co-cultures in the United States. This line of scholarly inquiry is valuable in identifying specific communicative practices that consistently emerge from the experiences of several different marginalized groups. The lived experiences described in this book have the potential for direct application, while also creating a context for further theoretical and research efforts. This final chapter will evaluate co-cultural theory, reflect on its relationship to existing research on communication and culture, and discuss implications for future research on, and application of, co-cultural theory.

Evaluating Co-cultural Theory

The primary objective of the series of research projects encompassed in this book is to establish a theoretical framework to gain insight into the communicative experiences of different co-cultural groups. Nevertheless, once the "logic of these practices" (de Certeau, 1984, p. xv) has been recognized, scholars can begin to launch further inquiries into this phenomenon. The identification and explication of six interrelated factors that influence the transactional process by which co-cultural group members adopt communication orientations are meaningful advances in that they offer a conceptualization that promotes a deeper understanding of how (and suggests why) those without societal power communicate. With the humanistic standards for evaluating theories (discussed by Griffin, 1997) as a guideline, the effectiveness of co-cultural theory can be measured by examining its ability to accomplish some or all of the following functions: create understanding, clarify values, stimulate agreement, inspire aesthetic appreciation, and change society. The relative strengths of a co-cultural perspective can be described by these criteria.

Strengths

The first criterion of a "good" humanistic theory is that it offers fresh insight into human communication. Co-cultural theory is unique in that it originates from the lived experiences of persons usually marginalized in traditional research and theory. The standpoint of co-cultural group members, reflecting their communicative experiences within dominant society ("outsiders within"), gives scholars a new perspective from which to consider communication processes. A co-cultural viewpoint encourages a scholarly position that acknowledges communication practices within a historical context of cultural power imbalances. Co-cultural communication theory offers a unique perspective of the phenomenon of cultural communication by attempting to reveal the common practices of those persons traditionally muted in dominant societal structures. Whereas earlier research focused on the communication of a particular group (e.g., African Americans, women, gays and lesbians), co-cultural theory provides a framework to explore the commonalities between and among groups.

Constructive humanistic theory also promotes a clarification of values. Instead of attempting to maintain an objective stance like their scientific counterparts, humanists create knowledge that readily brings people's values into consciousness. An important component of exposing the values inherent in knowledge-seeking activities is a continual examination of the power relationships inherent in all communication. The theoretical framework described in this book encourages a reflective stance for both dominant and co-cultural group members. In this regard, persons may reveal how their previously seen but unobserved communicative behavior attempts to reinforce, enhance, or challenge existing power cultures at a variety of levels (personal, social, organizational, institutional). Co-cultural theory also champions an "ethical imperative" for theorists that "grant[s] others that occur in your construction the same autonomy you practice constructing them" (Krippendorff, 1989, p. 83). Phenomenological inquiry, regarded as a critical method, provides an ontological space in which such a conceptualization is advanced. A standpoint infrastructure, which acknowledges the diversity of lived experiences in its approach, is also significant in promoting this ambitious objective.

A third standard for theories grounded in a humanistic paradigm involves a community of agreement among like-minded scholars. "Good" theory is identified by the amount of support and quality of comments that it generates from others. Although co-cultural theory does not profess to contain a series of testable hypotheses, it does contain a significant amount of new insight into the ways in which culture and communication are viewed. In this regard, it holds a certain degree of heuristic value; it should stimulate the thinking of others interested in this field of study. As described in great detail throughout this book, co-cultural theory promotes an outsider-within perspective of communication, one that is largely absent in traditional examinations. The theoretical framework presented in

Chapter 5 fosters several directions for future research (these will be discussed in a subsequent section of this chapter). Time will tell to what extent co-cultural theory generates further analyses among communication scholars.

A fourth evaluation question asks: Does co-cultural theory contain aesthetic appeal? Convincing humanistic theories, as other artistic endeavors, take a form that captures the imagination of readers just as much as its content does. Although the construction of a co-cultural model as "art" is debatable, its form does encourage others to view an age-old event (communication) through a new set of lenses. To its benefit, co-cultural theory is simple to understand, yet simultaneously complex in its descriptions and explorations of communication processes. Through its explication of experiences, co-cultural theory encourages opportunities for theorists, practitioners, and students to experience epiphanies concerning co-cultural communication. Through such personal analysis, perceptions of reality become clearer through a sudden intuitive realization. Such characterizations typically reflect accomplishments with a certain degree of aesthetic appeal.

A crucial aspect of any humanistic theory, including co-cultural theory, is its ability to generate societal change. How does the theory work, if at all, toward promoting social reform on personal, social, organizational, or institutional levels? Theory, according to Gergen (1982),

> [should have] the capacity to challenge the guiding assumptions of the culture, to raise fundamental questions regarding contemporary social life, to foster reconsideration of that which is "taken for granted," and thereby to generate fresh alternatives for social action. (p. 109)

Co-cultural theory holds the promise of generating social change in the lives of scholars, students, and practitioners; this promise was made apparent through the empowering process experienced by co-researchers during capta collection (especially focus groups). Co-cultural group members, whose narratives were crucial to the development of co-cultural theory, found a sense of renewed strength as they gave consciousness to their intricate communicative practices when interacting within dominant society. Through its descriptions of communication adaptability, co-cultural theory reveals the spirit of human creativity and perseverance. Such an explication of the intricate process by which co-cultural group members communicate within dominant societal structures often generates a keen sense of pride and accomplishment for underrepresented group members. The acknowledgment of this phenomenon, in discussions of theory as well as their personal lives, fosters a sense of empowerment that increases the likelihood of personal, social, and/or organizational change.

Generating societal reform, especially from the perspective of those persons traditionally marginalized in dominant societal structures, involves a lengthy, intricate process. Nevertheless, most scholars and practitioners alike believe that effective communication is a key component in promoting understanding among the diverse groups in our nation. An acute awareness of intergroup relations, in terms of how they reflect intersections of culture, power, and communication, is a decisive step toward societal change for co-cultural and dominant group members.

Limitations

On the basis of the abbreviated review and application of the evaluation criterion for humanistic theories, the co-cultural theory developed in this book has several strong points. Nevertheless, the theory as it stands in present form does have several limitations. From its inception, co-cultural theory has been reviewed by leading scholars in the communication field through several different review processes. These evaluations occurred at different stages of theory development and were conducted by at least 15 blind reviewers using a series of different conference, journal, and book review processes. Many of their comments resulted in a "tightening" process that ultimately generated a more effective theoretical framework. But other critiques, albeit somewhat resolved, still remain relevant as limitations of co-cultural theory. Ideally, the identification of such issues will lead to subsequent attention and ultimately improved effectiveness.

Methodological Limitations

An inherent limitation of co-cultural communication theory involves its use of phenomenological methodology. Whereas some attention was given in Chapter 1 to the criticisms of traditional research on culture and communication, phenomenological inquiry is not without its critics. Many of the general limitations associated with more humanistic, qualitative research are applicable to the description of co-cultural theory. First, the theoretical model presented in this book emerged from the descriptions of lived experiences of less than 100 co-cultural group members. Social scientists will undoubtedly question the selection process of co-researchers with regard to obtaining a random sample base. Moreover, challenges regarding the theory's limited generalizability, in light of a small sample, are also possible. Questions indicating the limitations of a phenomenological inquiry are often posed with regard to its limited generalizability: How representative are the behaviors? How widespread is any given communicative practice? Is any particular finding idiosyncratic?

Second, the theory involves an interpretation of co-cultural experiences through a scholarly lens; therefore, an ideological bias is introduced into the analysis. Through the rigor of phenomenology, several mechanisms (e.g., bracketing, imaginative free variation, self-reflexive) were employed to provide a discursive space for muted voices to be heard. Moreover, conscious attempts were made to include co-researchers in meaningful ways at each phase of the phenomenological inquiry process (description, reduction, and interpretation). These practices notwithstanding, the ultimate value of co-cultural theory still hinges on the author's interpretation, a distinct potential limitation inherent in critical [subjective] methodologies.

The criticisms of critical and interpretative work, such as those articulated above, have long been the impetus for regarding qualitative work as less "valuable" than more traditional social endeavors. Interesting enough, however, the ways in which the co-cultural communication model emerged (described in Chapter 5) may also be evaluated as limiting, from the perspective of certain phenomenology scholars. As Hyde and Smith (1979) explain, "The meanings of human existence, as it develops in and through interpretive understanding, always occurs within the hermeneutical situation" (p. 353). "Pure phenomenology" (Husserl, 1962) involves interpretations that remain in a set of specifically acknowledged life experiences. Whenever thematic explications are removed from the hermeneutical situation from which they emerged, they lose some of their meaning in the process (Hyde & Smith, 1979). The general description of the process by which co-cultural group members adopt specific communication orientations, according to this perspective, is limited in that the description is detached from the lived experiences from which meaning was originally situated. Although criticized by some, the move toward establishing relationships between lived experience and the structures that emerge from those experiences is consistent with other phenomenological directives (Merleau-Ponty, 1964; Warnick, 1979). In any case, the limitations posed by some scholars as inherent in the particular methodologies of initial co-cultural theory research will be considered in the discussions of future research implications toward the end of this chapter.

Limitations of Conceptualization

Several "points in progress" are acknowledged about the emergence of a new theoretical model of co-cultural communication. Whereas these issues remain in question and thus limit the general effectiveness of the theory, they also serve as the catalysts for future research inquiries into co-cultural communication. For instance, one limitation of the theoretical conceptualization of co-cultural communication is the apparent overlapping of communicative practices and factors influencing the adoption of various communication orientations. The bulk of Chapter 4 focused on describing, in some detail, more than 25 different communicative practices, some of which seemed similar or, in the least, subsets of other strategies. Variations of how co-cultural group members deal with stereotypes, for example, may encourage such criticism. How different are the practices of dispelling stereotypes and dissociating from certain stereotypical behaviors? As described in Chapters 4 and 5, dispelling stereotypes is consistent with a nonassertive accommodation orientation and involve countering existing co-cultural stereotypes through being oneself. Dissociating, in comparison, describes instances in which co-cultural group members make a concerted effort to avoid any behavior typically associated with their co-cultural identity to distance themselves from other group members (aggressive assimilation orientation). Some critics may perceive these communicative practices as largely the same and suggest that such a differentiation unnecessarily increases the complexity of strategy construction while ultimately reducing the merit of such a conceptualization. Similar critiques of the co-cultural practices of extensive preparation and overcompensating, bargaining and developing positive face, and other tactics are conceivable.

Nevertheless, it is imperative to note that the communicative practices described in Chapter 4 emerged directly from the oral narratives offered by a diverse collection of co-cultural group members. Distinctions, albeit sometimes diminutive, were given consciousness in the identification and explication of practices to reflect particulars made by co-cultural group members. Since this theoretical framework derives from the standpoint of these traditionally marginalized group members, such distinctions are important (although they may seem contrived or insignificant to some readers).

Moreover, some critical communication scholars may take issue with the apparent irony of using one factor, communication approach, in the conceptualization of a co-cultural communication theoretical framework. According to some, the arrangement of communication approaches—nonassertive, assertive, and aggressive—represents a traditional, dominant-group perspective that is paradoxical to interpret the communication styles descended from co-cultural group members' experiences. Some communication scholars (e.g., Kochman, 1990) maintain that perception of what constitutes nonassertiveness, assertiveness, and aggressiveness differs between dominant and co-cultural group members. Others, such as Buzzanell (1994), assert that such classifications of communication behavior give privilege to assertiveness and, to a lesser extent, aggressiveness, behavior traditionally associated with dominant group members. The effectiveness of nonassertiveness, used strategically by co-cultural group members and others, is connoted as weak, passive, or unsubstantial.

It is important to recognize that a communication approach, as a factor influencing the communicative practices of co-cultural group members, emerged from their descriptions of how they communicate with others. In this regard, the designation of what constitutes nonassertive, assertive, and aggressive behavior is derived from the descriptions of co-cultural group members. The application of the concepts of nonassertiveness, assertiveness, and aggressiveness within co-cultural theory, however, is made with a specific consciousness of the criticisms articulated by critical communication scholars. Some suggest that dominant structures can never be used to accurately portray and characterize co-cultural group experiences. I would contend, however, that an oppositional reading of some communication concepts that originated from a dominant group standpoint can prove to be beneficial in such a conceptualization. This is especially possible when the concepts are deconstructed and subsequently reconstructed from alternate perspectives. Such is the case with the arrangement of nonassertive, assertive, and aggressive communication approaches used in co-cultural theory. Throughout the narratives in this book are countless illustrations of instances when co-cultural group members manipulated dominant group perceptions of what constitutes nonassertive, assertive, and aggressive practices to achieve certain goals. In this regard, "the master's tools" can, in fact, be used for any number of goals, including the "dismantling of the master's house."

The conception of six interdependent factors related to the process of adopting specific communication orientations is an important step in the development of co-cultural theory. A deeper analysis of how the influential factors—preferred outcome, field of experience, abilities, situational context, perceived costs and rewards, and communication approach—converge during co-cultural communication is also pivotal in advancing understanding. Fostering a framework that suggests how clusters of communicative practices comprise nine different communication orientations represents such progress. Such a development is crucial to the basic tenets of co-cultural theory as it illuminates the interdependence and intricate complexities associated with co-cultural communication. In this regard, the six factors assist in explicating the process by which co-cultural group members experience co-cultural communication:

> Situated within a particular *field of experience* that governs their perceptions of the *costs and rewards* associated with, as well as their *ability* to engage in, various communication practices, co-cultural group members will strategically select communication orientations—based on their *preferred outcomes* and *communication approaches*—to fit the circumstances of a specific *situation*.

This general explanation represents a substantial effort in capturing the essence of co-cultural communication. Although more specific characterizations of this phenomenon are suggested, such as those suggested through the application of communication orientation and the potential costs and rewards associated with each, such representations should not be construed as a definitive model of co-cultural communication. One of the limitations to such a theoretical conceptualization, if taken as a measure of effectiveness rather than a measure of meaning (Crow, 1981), is that it jeopardizes the inclusion and significance of various co-cultural standpoints within the framework. For instance, strategies were grouped along two continua (separation, accommodation, or assimilation and nonassertive, assertive, or aggressive) to identify nine communication orientations. Arrangement of communicative practices in these different orientations was based on the descriptions of co-cultural group members' preferred outcomes and communication approaches. Nevertheless, at times distinctions between groupings (e.g., dispelling stereotypes as an assertive or nonassertive behavior) were difficult to ascertain. When discrepancies arose, the original transcripts of co-cultural narratives were consulted and given preference to the confines delineated in what traditionally has been used to constitute different approaches and/or outcomes.

Representative of the vast amount of human ingenuity, co-cultural group members have developed an array of communicative practices when interacting with dominant group members. It also appears that persons can adopt certain practices to accomplish one or more outcomes contingent on the situational context. A case in point occurred during the conceptualization of the nine co-cultural communication orientations that emerged when drawing associations among influential factors (see Figure 5.2). Two co-cultural communicative practices, communicating self and intragroup networking, were virtually impossible to distinguish as tactics solely inherent in assertive separation or assertive accommodation orientation. Even on closer scrutiny, these two communicative practices appeared to be used with equal effectiveness toward both preferred outcomes. It is feasible that other co-cultural practices, although not initially identified as such, also have the likelihood to be orchestrated in different ways by co-cultural group members. Such an ability is another testament of human creativity, as initially discussed by Stanback and Pearce (1981).

A final criticism of co-cultural theory is one that displays the opportunity for further application beyond co-cultural group members as defined throughout this book. Co-cultural theory derives from various marginalized groups in our society, including women, people of color, gays, lesbians, bisexuals, and those of lower socioeconomic status. Once the lived descriptions of these persons were collected, reviewed, and interpreted, common patterns of communication emerged that materialized as equally appropriate for other co-cultural groups (the elderly, young people, religious minorities, and persons with disabilities). Nevertheless, additional scrutiny from dominant group members surfaced that centers around their perceptions that *they also use co-cultural communicative practices in different situations.* A pertinent question concerning an apparent limitation of co-cultural theory arises from this line of inquiry: Are the practices and communication orientations explicated here exclusive to a co-cultural standpoint? Or do they speak to a more general human communication perspective inclusive of both co-cultural and dominant group members?

The Central Issues of Culture and Power

An issue that is central to the emergence of co-cultural theory is the inextricable relationship between culture, power, and communication. One strength of this emerging theoretical framework is that it seeks to expose the intricate ways in which culture and power influence the process of communication. As articulated earlier, marginalized group members have a constructive vantage point to these processes since they typically have a working knowledge of both dominant and co-cultural group structures.

The preliminary research reported here appears to indicate that co-cultural group members, despite organizational, social, or personal status or power, continue to consciously select specific communicative practices when communicating within dominant societal structures. These behaviors are warranted, from a co-cultural standpoint, since co-cultural group members perceive their existence in dominant society from an "outsider-within" perspective. Nevertheless, the communicative practices described here might also apply to other persons who experience a more temporary co-cultural position on the basis of a lack of education or work experience. Therefore, a young European American heterosexual employee in an entry-level position may choose similar communicative practices when interacting in an organizational setting. Although the extent and pervasiveness of this type of subjective position are drastically different from others' position based on permanent characteristics such as ethnicity and gender, similar power dynamics may be employed. This line of reasoning is consistent with two ideas discussed earlier: (a) dominant or nondominant status can change depending on the saliency of one's cultural position in a specific context, and (b) muteness, the process by which one is made inarticulate, is not a fixed condition.

Defining culture more broadly promotes an understanding of how some persons, typically regarded as dominant group members, experience "transient powerlessness" and adopt co-cultural communicative practices. From its inception, co-cultural theory sought to discover commonalities in the ways in which humans resist oppressive structures. The implication that dominant group members, whose cultural field of experience includes instances when they were marginalized, might respond in similar ways is confirmation of this basic paragon.

Loden and Rosener (1991) distinguish between two dimensions of cultural diversity. The paradigm that they suggest promotes a conceptualization of culture crucial to understanding the dynamics of co-cultural theory. Loden and Rosener differentiate between the primary dimension of diversity that is more permanent in nature and secondary dimension that inherently possesses the ability to change over one's life experiences. The primary dimension of diversity has six levels: age, ethnicity, gender, physical abilities or qualities, race, and sexual or affection orientation. These attributes are regarded as more invariable than those included in the secondary dimension. The the secondary dimension of diversity has, but is not limited to, several levels: educational background, geographic location, marital status, military experience, parental status, religious beliefs, socioeconomic status, and work experience. Those persons whose lived experiences are marginalized by the dominant group perspective because of one of these levels are the principal focus of co-cultural communication theory. Initial descriptions of co-cultural theory were inclusive of only one aspect present in the secondary dimension of diversity: socioeconomic status. Applicability of the framework for religious minorities was made apparent in subsequent reflection on the multidimensional process of co-cultural communication.

Loden and Rosener's (1991) work in the area of diversity makes it apparent that marginalization of group members based on other levels represented in the secondary dimension may also be described within a co-cultural perspective. Clearly all the characteristics of both dimensions help to shape the self-image of persons and consequently their communication. Depending on the varying levels of salience, a person's communicative behavior may be stimulated by one or more components of a multileveled cultural identity. European American heterosexual males who experience an outsider's perspective when assuming an entry-level organizational position may embrace a co-cultural group positioning. This capacity may be the result of subordination on the basis of their age, lack of education, or lack of work experience. In this regard, these persons may accept a transient co-cultural perspective in their attempts to regain dominant group status.

Whereas these instances reflect similarities to the primary dimensions of co-cultural diversity, it is important to acknowledge that the pervasiveness of societal oppression based on these characteristics varies greatly. However analogous in certain instances, the field of experiences of co-cultural group members whose identity is related to a more lasting state of oppression is quite different from those dominant group members who experience fleeting marginalization amid a history (and future) of privilege. A realization of their social status in a historical context forces co-cultural group members to adopt various communication orientations in ways different from dominant group members. These differences are grounded in a person's field of experience that shapes the ways in which other influential factors (preferred outcome, abilities, perceived costs and rewards, situation, communication approach) are understood. Although dominant group members may use co-cultural communicative practices in different instances, the process of selecting, implementing, and evaluating practices is different from marginalized group members on the basis of their divergent fields of experiences. This point is best understood by the comments of Lakoff (1995): "However identical communication strategies appear to superficial inspection, in fact they have different meaning because of the power bases from which the strategies are enacted" (p. 46).

In short, co-cultural theory is designed to speak to the lived communicative experiences of those persons traditionally marginalized within dominant societal structures. Although some processes may lend insight into a more general approach to communication (especially as influenced by power dynamics), the primarily descriptive focus is on the perpetual process of co-cultural communication among those persons whose life experiences never progress beyond an outsider-within position.

Implications for Future Co-cultural Research

The ability of co-cultural theory to apply to more general communication research, as suggested above, represents one of several interesting directions for future research. Co-cultural theory may provide insight into scholarly inquiries that seek to acknowledge power disparity in interpersonal communication. Given the broadly defined notion of culture suggested earlier, it appears that a co-cultural theoretical framework may be a point of initiation for researchers who advance the fundamental belief that all interpersonal communication is, in essence, intercultural communication (e.g., Orbe & Wilcoxson, 1995). Co-cultural theory provides a framework for research and theory that examines all communication, not simply those traditionally designated as intercultural, from a cultural perspective. In this regard, the saliency of issues related to cultural identity negotiated by those involved in the interactive setting can be viewed as the determining consideration about which communication is regarded as interpersonal or co-cultural in nature.

The most potentially fertile area for future research related to co-cultural theory, however, lies within the area of co-cultural communication itself. In the spirit of cultural or critical approaches, such as muted-group and standpoint theories, co-cultural theory lends itself nicely to a continued line of inquiry that gives predilection to the significance of an inclusion of underrepresented voices in communication research and theory. Using the foundations set forth by muted-group and standpoint theories, co-cultural theory provides a conceptual framework that focuses on the commonalities of oppressed groups while simultaneously acknowledging the great diversity of lived experiences within and among such groups.

Co-cultural theory is not a "totalizing theory" that represents the definitive source on culture and communication. Instead, like standpoint theory, it represents (Smith, 1992) a continued point "of inquiry, always ongoing, opening things up, discovering . . . an inquiry relevant to the politics and practices of progressive struggle" (p. 8).

From the conceptual model presented in co-cultural theory, a variety of future research possibilities exists. These endeavors further extend our understanding of the implications of culture and power in communication processes. One clear direction for future research involves subsequent exploration of co-cultural communication orientations and the practices that comprise them. Currently, more than 25 communicative practices have been identified and explicated regarding nine primary communication orientations. Given the basic notion that the variety of these co-cultural communicative practices is limited only by human ingenuity, several research questions can be investigated: What additional co-cultural communicative practices, or variations of current practices, exist? How do the co-cultural practices identified through other research efforts reinforce, complement, or contradict the various strategies described here? How do new practices (or innovative variations of existing practices) correspond to the nine primary communication orientations employed by co-cultural group members?

As stated in Chapter 1, a basic premise of co-cultural theory relates to the assumption that some commonalities exist among the ways in which people endure structures that oppress their existence. The co-cultural theoretical framework described throughout this book was successful in that it could establish a general characterization of communication processes from the perspective of marginalized group members. One of the strengths of the framework is that it appears to speak to the collective commonalities of co-cultural group members in general, while also providing space for the specific experiences of different groups (African Americans, women, Latino Americans, gays, lesbians, bisexuals, those from a lower socioeconomic background, etc.). Whereas there is certainly no "hierarchy of oppression" (Lorde, 1984), the ways in which oppressive structures are employed do vary among sexist, racist, classist, heterosexist, and other forms of subjugation. On the basis of any number of levels, differences in co-cultural communication orientations may be notably apparent when people of color, gays and lesbians, and women are considered. Additional research that draws on the commonalities established in the co-cultural theoretical framework general model and reveals variations among specific co-cultural groups may provide a deeper understanding of the intricate relationship among culture, power, and communication. These issues and others can be explored by using co-cultural communication theory to return to the microlevel everyday practices of marginalized group members from which the framework emerged. In essence, these future projects constitute an extension of the hermeneutic spiral in phenomenological inquiry.

Initial definitions of co-culture and co-cultural communication included a discussion of how the complexity of otherness affects intergroup communication. The notion of "co-cultural oppression" was introduced to describe instances in which additionally marginalized group members were in a context that also placed them in a position of privilege. Examples of co-cultural oppression include racism among women, classism in the gay community, and sexism among people of color. Future research inquiries may use the foundation of co-cultural theory—grounded conceptually in muted-group and standpoint theories—to explore how co-cultural group members function as both the "target and vehicle" (Foucault, 1979, p. 102) of oppressive communication. Although this area of research has generated limited attention in the field of communication, co-cultural theory encourages a conceptual stance by which "all groups possess varying amounts of penalty and privilege in one historically created system" (Collins, 1990, p. 172). Research that uses the framework established here to explore the communicative practices beyond the monolithic category of "other" will undoubtedly reveal additional insight into these intricate processes. One avenue of research involves the ways in which those persons regarded as dominant group members communicate with co-cultural group members.

Research inquiries that explore the ways in which both dominant and co-cultural group members simultaneously negotiate meaning within dominant structures is valuable to gaining a multidimensional perspective on co-cultural communication. Scholarly inquiries along these lines encourage a shift from research that places the responsibility of communication effectiveness primarily on the shoulders of co-cultural group members to one that is shared among both dominant and co-cultural group members. Moreover, several thought-provoking lines of research questions, as they relate specifically to the co-cultural communication process, can be explored: What are the immediate and long-term implications of adopting different orientations toward intergroup relations? What communicative practices contribute to maintaining a power imbalance? What conditions or orientations might contribute to a relationship based on equality rather than inequality?

A final consideration of additional research in co-cultural communication involves the selection process of communicative practices. An especially fruitful line of inquiry for future examination concerns the six influential factors of co-cultural communication described in Chapter 5. Additional scholarly inquiry can extend our understanding of how each of these eclectic factors directly and indirectly influences the consideration, implementation, and evaluation—and the subsequent reconsideration, reimplementation, and reevaluation—of a broad array of communicative practices. What additional insights are possible for research that focuses on the idea of field of experience, perceived costs and rewards, abilities, communication approach, preferred outcome, and situational context? The focus of such inquiries should include the distinct ways in which these factors are synchronously negotiated with dominant group members in a specific set of circumstances. Of equal importance, are these research undertakings that attempt to determine the interconnectedness of factors. As demonstrated by intersections of several factors (resulting in the conceptualization of various co-cultural communication orientations), such thematic associations promote an advanced understanding of the "hows" and "whys" of co-cultural communication. The number of possibilities for future research in this avenue is infinite. Ultimately, research along this line of inquiry may foster the development of a more comprehensive model of co-cultural communication that strengthens our awareness of the phenomenon without disregarding the diverse standpoints of co-cultural group members.

"Setting in Motion" a Co-cultural Dialectic

Via a phenomenological methodology, the theoretical concepts presented throughout this book emerged thematically from the descriptions of co-researchers' lived experiences as their function in dominant societal structures. A conscious decision was made to employ a phenomenological framework on the basis of the perceived strengths inherent in a methodology capable of a rigorous, inductive, interpretative inquiry. Nevertheless, this perspective does not say that a traditional social scientific approach to studying culture and communication has less to contribute toward greater insight into co-cultural communication. As articulated by Merleau-Ponty (1964) nearly 34 years ago, phenomenology can complement, as well as be complemented by, more conventional social scientific methodologies. "As soon as we distinguish, alongside objective science of language, a phenomenology of speech, we set in a motion a dialectic through which the two disciplines open communications" (p. 86).

One way to "set in motion" a dialectic that opens the possibility of additional insight into the process by which co-cultural group members adopt various communication orientations while functioning in dominant societal structures is to acknowledge how existing communication research—both from a social scientific and rhetorical perspective—can potentially complement the theoretical framework presented here.

Two specific theoretical concepts that can lend insight into the process of co-cultural communication are "Rhetorical Sensitivity" by Hart and Burks (1972) and "Communication Accommodation Theory (CAT)" by Giles and colleagues (Giles, Mulac, Bradac, & Johnson, 1987).

Rhetorical Sensitivity

Communication researcher Roderick Hart and his colleagues' work on Rhetorical Sensitivity (Hart & Burks, 1972; Hart, Carlson, & Eadie, 1980) offers an interesting vantage point to explore co-cultural communication. According to Hart et al. (1980), this communication concept is "distinctive because it champions tentativeness or rigidity, prizes symbolic solutions to human dilemmas and appreciates the complexity of social exchange" (p. 1).

In this regard, the notion of rhetorical sensitivity is a valuable theory as it relates to the discussion here since it recognizes the diversity of co-cultural group members and the complexity of the communication process.

Hart and Burks (1972) identified three categories of communicators that provide some insight into co-cultural communication. The first type of communicator Hart and Burks describe is the noble self. Co-cultural group members who are in this category tend to stick to their own ideals with little variation and adjustment to others. Low self-monitors (Snyder, 1974), these persons communicate in ways that suit their needs, with little or no attention to dominant group perceptions. Within a co-cultural theoretical perspective, noble selves might describe those co-cultural group members as adopting an aggressive accommodation and aggressive separation orientation.

At the other end of the spectrum are co-cultural group members labeled rhetorical reflectors (Hart & Burks, 1972). These persons are considered high self-monitors (Snyder, 1974), modeling themselves after dominant group expectations in virtually every circumstance. Adopting an extreme receiver-orientation perspective, rhetorical reflectors communicate what others want to hear and rarely express personal viewpoints. According to Hart and Burks, this type of communicator typically is energized for manipulative purposes or engaged out of a lack of self-confidence. Drawing from a co-cultural communication perspective, rhetorical reflectors can be seen in nonassertive, assertive, and aggressive assimilation orientations. Varying degrees may also be applicable to those co-cultural group members who assume a nonassertive accommodation or separation orientation.

The third style of communicator, one that is seen as a combination of the noble self and rhetorical reflector, is termed *rhetorical sensitivity*. Co-cultural group members in this category take an assertive approach to communication, balancing a concern for themselves with a concern for others (co-cultural and dominant group members). Hart et al. (1980) describe five characteristics of rhetorically sensitive co-cultural group members. The first characteristic is an acceptance of personal complexity, along with a keen awareness of the complex network of selves—only some of which are socially visible—and human unpredictability. The second attribute of rhetorical sensitivity is avoidance of communicative rigidity. These persons refuse to opt for the same role without regard to situational context and typically engage in interpersonal or inventional flexibility. A third characteristic of this type of communicator is an interaction consciousness, in which co-cultural group members balance self and others' interests. The fourth element of a rhetorically sensitive communicator is an appreciation of the communicability of ideas. In other words, these persons understand the varying levels of "appropriateness" in different communication contexts and govern themselves accordingly. The final attribute is a tolerance for inventional searching, with the realization that an idea can be communicated in many different ways with varying degrees of success. In short, a rhetorically sensitive person is a person who willingly characterizes himself or herself as (Hart & Burks, 1972) "an undulating, fluctuating entity, always unsure, always guessing, continually weighing potential communicative decisions" (p. 90).

By definition, rhetorically sensitive co-cultural group members find themselves drawing from each of the nine primary communication orientations described above. Depending on the saliency of influential factors in any given situational context, these co-cultural group members will consciously consider which communication style will elicit the greatest results with the lowest costs. Explicit in the descriptions of rhetorical sensitivity is a presumption that these persons combine the strengths affiliated with the noble self and rhetorical reflector to create an "ideal communication type." Nevertheless, the work in this area also suggests that rhetorical sensitivity includes communication by one's noble self and rhetorical reflector when circumstances warrant their effectiveness. With respect to co-cultural communication, it is my contention that each type of communicator is needed to provoke change among the varying levels within dominant societal structures. Co-cultural members who primarily communicate out of their noble selves are effective when others cannot be; the same is true for rhetorical reflectors. In this regard, no one ideal type of communicator exists. Each communicator type—noble self, rhetorical reflector, and rhetorically sensitive person—is "ideal" depending on how each co-cultural group member perceives the six influential factors inherent in strategy selection.

It is important to recognize that, in its discussions, the work on rhetorical sensitivity does not explicitly acknowledge the power dynamics associated with culture in society. With respect to its application to co-cultural communication theory, rhetorical sensitivity does contribute a basic topology that lends itself to the ideas described in this book. It also emphasizes the situational nature of communication and places a priority on acknowledging "suitably complex schemes of rhetorical invention" (Hart et al., 1980, p. 21). The theoretical framework depicting the specific communicative practices selected by co-cultural group members appears to extend the ideas of Hart et al. as they directly relate to the standpoint of co-cultural group experiences. Consistent with the following rhetorical perspective (Hart et al., 1980), co-cultural communication theory promotes a more sophisticated conceptualization of communication types specific to co-cultural group experiences: "The rhetorical perspective has long stressed the prodigious demands placed on us during communicative encounters—the ability to judge carefully, the willingness to be quiet occasionally, and the advisability of rejecting easy communicative bromides" (p. 21).

Communication Accommodation Theory

Communication Accommodation Theory (CAT, Giles et al., 1987) focuses on the "social cognitive processes mediating individuals' perceptions of the environment and their communicative behaviors" (p. 14). Specifically, CAT examines the motivations and constraints associated with speech convergence and divergence during interpersonal interactions. These two conceptual stances, when viewed via a co-cultural communication perspective, are closely aligned with the preferred outcomes of assimilation and separation, respectively. Convergence, according to Giles et al., is a communication strategy by which individuals adapt to one another's behavior. Divergence, in contrast, refers to ways in which speakers accentuate communication differences between themselves and others. Whereas convergence is most clearly paralleled with assimilation and divergence with separation, CAT does describe possible convergent efforts in which both parties "meet midway linguistically" (Giles et al., 1987, p. 16), that could be a form of accommodation.

Some distinct similarities exist between co-cultural theory and CAT; the opportunity to compare and contrast these similarities may provide additional insights that might advance both theories. Like the concepts associated with the theory of Rhetorical Sensitivity described earlier, CAT does not centrally involve how power dynamics (at interpersonal, organizational, or societal levels) affect intergroup communication. Instead, both parties involved in the interaction are assumed to be communicating on equal levels—an assumption in direct conflict with a co-cultural communication perspective. Consequently, much of the insight generated through research in the area of CAT is problematic when exploring the communicative experiences of co-cultural group members functioning within dominant societal structures. A brief analysis of the reformulated propositions of CAT, as presented by Giles et al. (1987) will illustrate how these ideas negate the influence of societal power in interpersonal interactions.

These six propositions describe the various antecedents and consequences of convergence and divergence processes. Some hypotheses appear generally applicable to the lived experiences of co-cultural group members, especially those that describe the impact of social approval, perceived costs and rewards, and appropriate situational or identity definitions (Giles et al., 1987, pp. 36-37). Nevertheless, many propositions become problematic when acknowledging the "outsider-within" position of co-cultural group members in dominant societal structures. For instance, Proposition 3(e) (Giles et al., 1987) states that

> speakers will attempt to maintain their communication patterns, or even diverge away from their message recipients' speech and nonverbal behaviors when recipients . . . exhibit a stigmatized form, that is, a style that deviates from a valued norm which is consistent with speakers' expectations regarding recipient performance. (p. 37)

The use of certain terms such as "stigmatized form" and "style that deviates from a valued norm" indicate the presence of a clear standard—and subsequently substandard—form of communication. The perspective of CAT implicitly promotes the premise that all speakers and receivers enter interactions with similar opportunities to designate which forms of communication are valued and which are stigmatized as inappropriate. Co-cultural communication theory, with its grounding in muted-group theory, resists this idyllic notion. Instead, the framework described in this book is based on the notion that dominant group members largely construct communication structures that fail to reflect the lived experiences of those co-cultural group members. Over time, these communicative structures develop as the "valued norm" and the communication of those persons marginalized within dominant society is stigmatized as deviant.

Whereas CAT does acknowledge the role of organizational power (manager or subordinate dimension) as it relates to social approval and attempts at convergence or divergence (Giles et al., 1987, p. 22), it does not address the effects of dominant group institutional oppression on the daily life experiences of co-cultural group members. These shortcomings aside, CAT can provide additional insight into the intricacies of co-cultural communication. Similarly, the main ideas of CAT may be developed with a recognition of how dominant or co-cultural group power dynamics permeate interpersonal interactions.

Rhetorical Sensitivity and Communication Accommodation Theory represent two conceptual frameworks that, after some involved review, can lend insight into the co-cultural communication framework described throughout this book. Although the possible contributions of these two theories were highlighted, other avenues of exploration are possible. For instance, existing scholarship concerning assimilation, accommodation, separation (Golden & Rieke, 1971; Parrillo, 1996), strategic interaction (Goffman, 1959), Social Exchange Theory (Kelley, 1979; Thibaut & Kelley, 1959), self-monitoring (Snyder, 1974), communication approach (Alberti & Emmons, 1990; Wilson, Hantz, & Hanna, 1995), compliance-gaining strategies (Dillard, 1990) and interaction goals (Beniot, 1990; Wilson & Putnam, 1990) all appear in the process by which co-cultural group members come to select specific communication orientations. Research inquiries that extend the hermeneutic spiral and return the thematic conclusions inherent in co-cultural theory to the persons from which the concepts emerged can further explore the communicative complexities within and between these groups. These studies can also gain insight from existing research on these co-cultural groups (Braithwaite, 1990; Gong, 1994; Hecht et al., 1993; Hecht et al., 1990; Kochman, 1990; Meade, 1996; Philipsen, 1975; Spradlin, 1995; Woods, 1993). Such a multiperspective of exploring the intricate process of co-cultural communication is necessary to advance understanding beyond that of cursory discernment.

Conclusion

The co-cultural perspective described throughout this book is a manifestation of an evolving scholarly inquiry that began during my doctoral program. Naively, I surmised that fulfilling the requirements for my doctoral degree would answer the basic question of how those without societal power communicate with those who have access to societal power. As I completed my dissertation, however, a scholarly precept that was previously stored away materialized: "Good" research generates more questions than it answers. In this regard, co-cultural theory represents another level of understanding of how I understand the relationship between communication, culture, and power—it provides answers for some questions, while prompting additional related points of inquiry. "The closer one is to the phenomenon, the more likely one is to see internal differences" (Duster, 1993, p. 238). Such is the case for co-cultural communication. With a substantial theoretical framework in place, additional scholarly scrutiny—through both interpretative and social scientific perspectives—is needed to generate deeper understanding into the communicative experiences of specific co-cultural groups. Beyond advancing communication theory, this line of research also has the potential to promote greater understanding of intergroup relations in this country. Our ultimate understanding of co-cultural relations hinges on our abilities to understand the commonalities among groups without negating the differences between (and within) those groups. The concept of co-cultural communication is grounded in this idea and promotes, through the theoretical framework presented in this book, a means to come to understand the complex intersections of culture, power, and communication inherent in intergroup relations.

References

Alberti, R., & Emmons, M. (1990). *Your perfect right: A guide to assertive behavior.* San Luis Obispo, CA: Impact.

Anderson, E. (1990). *Streetwise: Race, class, and change in an urban community.* Chicago: University of Chicago Press.

Anderson, K., & Jack, D. C. (1991). Learning to listen: Interview techniques and analysis. In S. B. Gluck & D. Patai (Eds.), *Women's words: The feminist practice of oral history* (pp. 11-27). Boston: Routledge Kegan Paul.

Aptheker, B. (1989). *Tapestries of life: Women's work, women's consciousness, and the meaning of daily experience.* Amherst: University of Massachusetts Press.

Ardener, E. (1978). Some outstanding problems in the analysis of events. In G. Schwinner (Ed.), *The yearbook of symbolic anthropology* (pp. 103-121).

Ardener, S. (1975). *Perceiving women.* London: Malaby.

Ardener, S. (1978). *Defining females: The nature of women in society.* New York: John Wiley.

Arendt, H. (1986). Communicative power. In S. Lukes (Ed.), *Power* (pp. 59-74). New York: New York University Press.

Arliss, L. P., & Borisoff, D. J. (1993). *Women & men communicating: Challenges and changes.* New York: Holt, Rinehart & Winston.

Asante, M. K. (1991). Multiculturalism: An exchange. *American Scholar, 59,* 267-271.

Auden, W. H. (1967, October). A short defense of poetry. Paper presented at the annual meeting of the International PEN, Budapest, Hungary.

Ayers, K. (1994, April). *Life transitions: Exploring how retirement affects interpersonal communication.* Paper presented at the annual Women's Studies Conference, Indiana University at Kokomo, Kokomo, IN.

Banks, J. A. (1988). *Multiethnic education: Theory and practice* (2nd ed.). Boston: Allyn & Bacon.

Baxter, L. A., & Goldsmith, D. (1990). Cultural terms for communication events among some American high school adolescents. *Western Journal of Speech Communication, 54,* 377-394.

Beniot, P. J. (1990). The structure of interaction goals. In J. A. Anderson (Ed.), *Communication Yearbook 13* (pp. 407-416). Newbury Park, CA: Sage.

Biles, R., Shapiro, D., & Cummings, L. (1988). Casual accounts and managing organizational conflict. *Communication Research, 15*(4), 381-399.

Borisoff, D., & Merrill, L. (1992). *The power to communicate: Gender differences as barriers.* Prospect Heights, IL: Waveland.

Bradac, J. J., & Mulac, A. (1984). Attributional consequences of powerful and powerless speech styles in a crisis-intervention context. *Journal of Language and Social Psychology, 3*(1), 1-19.

Bradshaw, C. (1992). Beauty and the beast: On racial ambiguity. In M. P. Root (Ed.), *Racially mixed people in America* (pp. 77-88). Newbury, CA: Sage.

Braithwaite, D. O. (1990). From majority to minority: An analysis of cultural change from ablebodied to disabled. *International Journal of Intercultural Relations, 14,* 465-483.

Braithwaite, D. O. (1991). Just how much did that wheelchair cost?: Management of privacy boundaries by persons with disabilities. *Western Journal of Speech Communication, 55,* 254-274.

Brislin, R. (1993). *Understanding culture's influence on behavior.* Orlando, FL: Harcourt Brace.

Brown, P., & Levinson, S. (1978). Universals in language usage: Politeness phenomena. In E. N. Goody (Ed.), *Questions and politeness: Strategies in social interaction* (pp. 56-89). Cambridge, MA: Cambridge University Press.

Bucholtz, M. (1995). From mulatta to mestiza: Passing and the linguistic reshaping of ethnic identity. In K. Hall & M. Bucholtz (Eds.), *Gender articulated: Language and the socially constructed self* (pp. 351-374). Boston: Routledge Kegan Paul.

Buzzanell, P. (1994). Gaining a voice: Feminist organization communication theorizing. *Management Communication Quarterly, 7,* 339-383.

Campbell, K. K. (1986). Style and content in the rhetoric of early Afro-American feminists. *Quarterly Journal of Speech, 72,* 434-445.

Chesebro, J. W. (1981). *Gayspeak: Gay male and lesbian communication.* New York: Pilgrim.

Colaizzi, P. F. (1973). *Reflection and research in psychology.* Dubuque, IA: Kendall/Hunt.

Collier, M. J., Ribeau, S. A., & Hecht, M. L. (1986). Intracultural communication rules and outcomes within three domestic cultures. *International Journal of Intercultural Relations, 10,* 439-457.

Collins, P. H. (1986). Learning from the outsider within: The sociological significance of black feminist thought. *Social Problems, 33*(6), S14-S23.

Collins, P. H. (1989). The social construction of black feminist thought. *Signs, 4,* 745-773.

Collins, P. H. (1990). *Black feminist thought: Knowledge, consciousness, and the politics of empowerment*. Winchester, MA: Unwin Hyman.
Cooks, L. M., & Orbe, M. (1993). Beyond the satire: Selective exposure and selective perception in "In Living Color." *Howard Journal of Communication, 4*(3), 217-233.
Crow, B. (1981). Talking about films: A phenomenological study of film signification. In S. Deetz (Ed.), *Phenomenology in rhetoric and communication* (pp. 4-15). Washington, DC: University Press of America.
Cunningham, M. (1992, May/June). If you're queer and you're not angry in 1992, you're not paying attention; if you're straight it may be hard to figure out what all the shouting's about. *Mother Jones*, pp. 60-68.
Daley, M. (1978). *Gyn/ecology: The metaethics of radical feminism*. Boston: Beacon.
de Certeau, M. (1984). *The practice of everyday life* (S. Rendall, Trans.). Los Angeles: University of California Press.
Deetz, S. A. (1973). Words without things: Toward a social phenomenology of language. *Quarterly Journal of Speech, 59*, 40-51.
Deetz, S. A. (Ed.). (1981). *Phenomenology in rhetoric and communication*. Washington, DC: University Press of America.
Deetz, S. A. (1992). *Democracy in an age of corporate colonization: Developments in communication and the politics of everyday life*. Albany: State University of New York Press.
de Lauretis, T. (1984). *Feminist studies/critical studies*. Bloomington: Indiana University Press.
DeVito, J. A. (1995). *The interpersonal communication book*. New York: HarperCollins.
Dillard, J. P. (Ed.). (1990). *Seeking compliance: The production of interpersonal influence messages*. Scottsdale, AZ: Gorsuch Scarisbrick.
D'Souza, D. (1991). The new segregation on campus. *American Scholar, 59*, 17-30.
Duster, T. (1993). The diversity of California at Berkeley: An emerging reformulation of "competence" in an increasingly multicultural world. In B. W. Thompson & S. Tyagi (Eds.), *Beyond a dream deferred: Multicultural education and the politics of excellence* (pp. 231-255). Minneapolis: University of Minnesota Press.
Erni, J. (1989). Where is the "audience?": Discerning the (impossible) subject. *Journal of Communication, 13*(2), 30-42.
Etter-Lewis, G. (1991). Black women's life stories: Reclaiming self in narrative texts. In S. B. Gluck & D. Patai (Eds.), *Women's words: The feminist practice of oral history* (pp. 43-58). Boston: Routledge Kegan Paul.
Fant, O. D., Cohen, A., Cox, M., & Kanter, R. M. (1979). *A tale of "O": On being different*. Cambridge, MA: Goodmeasure.
Fiske, J. (1991). For cultural interpretation: A study of the culture of homelessness. *Critical Studies in Mass Communication, 8*, 455-474.
Flanagan, J. (1954). The critical incident technique. *Psychological Bulletin, 51*(4), 327-358.
Folb, E. (1994). Who's got the room at the top? Issues of dominance and nondominance in intracultural communication. In L. A. Samovar & R. E. Porter (Eds.), *Intercultural communication: A reader* (pp. 119-127). Belmont, CA: Wadsworth.
Ford-Ahmed, T. (1992, October). Exploring lived experiences of African American graduate women during an explosive week. Paper presented at the annual Midwest Popular Culture Association and the Midwest American Culture Association, Indianapolis, IN.

Ford-Ahmed, T., & Orbe, M. (1992, November). African American graduate students, their majority host institution and ethnic prejudice: A bright side? Paper presented at the annual meeting of the Speech Communication Association, Chicago, IL.

Foss, K. A., & Foss, S. K. (1994). Personal experience as evidence in feminist scholarship. *Western Journal of Communication, 58,* 39-43.

Foucault, M. (1979). *Discipline and punish: The birth of the prison* (A. Sheridan, Trans.). New York: Random House.

Frankenberg, R. (1993). *White women, race matters: The social construction of whiteness.* Minneapolis: University of Minnesota Press.

Gadamer, H. G. (1975). *Truth and method.* New York: Seabury.

Gergen, K. (1982). *Toward transformation in social knowledge.* New York: Springer-Verlag.

Giles, H., Mulac, A., Bradac, J. J., & Johnson, P. (1987). Speech accommodation theory: The first decade and beyond. In M. L. McLaughlin (Ed.), *Communication Yearbook 10* (pp. 13-48). Newbury Park, CA: Sage.

Gilligan, C. (1982). *In a different voice: Psychological theory and woman's development.* Cambridge, MA: Harvard University Press.

Gluck, S. B., & Patai, D. (Eds.). (1991). *Women's words: The feminist practice of oral history.* Boston: Routledge Kegan Paul.

Goffman, E. (1959). *The presentation of self in everyday life.* Garden City, NY: Doubleday.

Golden, J. C., & Rieke, R. D. (1971). *The rhetoric of black Americans.* Columbus, OH: Merrill.

Gong, G. (1994). When Mississippi Chinese talk. In A. Gonzalez, M. Houston, & V. Chen (Eds.), *Our Voices: Essays in culture, ethnicity, and communication* (pp. 133-139). Los Angeles, CA: Roxbury.

Gonzalez, A., Houston, M., & Chen, V. (Eds.). (1994). *Our voices: Essays in culture, ethnicity, and communication.* Los Angeles, CA: Roxbury.

Gregg, R. B. (1966). A phenomenologically oriented approach to rhetorical criticism. *The Central States Speech Journal, 17,* 83-90.

Griffin, E. (1997). *A first look at communication theory* (3rd ed.). New York: McGraw-Hill.

Gudykunst, W. B., & Hammer, M. R. (1987). The influence of ethnicity, gender, and dyadic composition on uncertainty reduction in initial interaction. *Journal of Black Studies, 18,* 191-214.

Hamilton, A. (1996, April 26). For middle-class blacks, success can mean turmoil. *Louisville (KY) Courier-Journal,* p. A4.

Harding, S. (Ed.). (1987). *Feminism & methodology.* Bloomington: Indiana University Press.

Harding, S. (1991). *Whose science? Whose knowledge? Thinking from women's lives.* Ithaca, NY: Cornell University Press.

Hart, R. P., & Burks, D. M. (1972). Rhetorical sensitivity and social interaction. *Speech Monographs, 39,* 75-91.

Hart, R. P., Carlson, R. E., & Eadie, W. F. (1980). Attitudes toward communication and the assessment of rhetorical sensitivity. *Communication Monographs, 47,* 1-22.

Hartsock, N. C. M. (1983). The feminist standpoint: Developing the ground for a specifically feminist historical materialism. In S. Harding & M. D. Hintikka (Eds.), *Discovering reality: Feminist perspectives on epistemology, metaphysics, methodology, and philosophy of science* (pp. 283-310). Boston: D. Reidel.

Hecht, M. L., Collier, M. J., & Ribeau, S. (1993). *African American Communication: Ethnic identity and cultural interpretation.* Newbury Park, CA: Sage.

Hecht, M. L., Ribeau, S., & Alberts, J. K. (1989). An Afro-American perspective on interethnic communication. *Communication Monographs, 56,* 385-410.

Hecht, M. L., Ribeau, S., & Sedano, M. V. (1990). A Mexican American perspective on interethnic communication. *International Journal of Intercultural Relations, 14,* 31-55.

Heilbrun, C., & Stimpson, C. (1975). Theories of feminist criticism: A dialogue. In J. Donovan (Ed.), *Feminist literary criticism* (pp. 61-73). Lexington: University Press of Kentucky.

Herring, S., Johnson, D. A., & DiBenedetto, T. (1995). "This discussion is going too far!": Male resistance to female participation on the internet. In K. Hall & M. Bucholtz (Eds.), *Gender articulated: Language and the socially constructed self* (pp. 67-96). Boston: Routledge Kegan Paul.

hooks, b. (1984). *From margin to center.* Boston: South End.

hooks, b. (1989). *Talking back: Thinking feminist, thinking black.* Boston: South End.

Houghton, C. (1995). Managing the body of labor: The treatment of reproduction and sexuality in a therapeutic institution. In K. Hall & M. Bucholtz (Eds.), *Gender articulated: Language and the socially constructed self* (pp. 121-142). Boston: Routledge Kegan Paul.

Houston, M. S. (1989). Feminist theory and black women's talk. *The Howard Journal of Communication, 1,* 187-194.

Houston, M. S. (1994). When black women talk to white women: Why dialogues are difficult. In A. Gonzalez, M. Houston, & V. Chen (Eds.), *Our Voices: Essays in culture, ethnicity, and communication* (pp. 133-139). Los Angeles, CA: Roxbury.

Houston, M. S., & Kramarae, C. (1991). Speaking from silence: Methods of silencing and of resistance. *Discourse & Society,* 2(4), 387-399.

Hull, G., Scott, P., & Smith, B. (1982). *All the women are white, all the blacks are men, but some of us are brave.* Old Westbury, NY: Feminist Press.

Hummert, M. L., Wiemann, J. M., & Nussbaum, J. F. (1994). *Interpersonal communication in older adulthood: Interdisciplinary theory and research.* Newbury Park, CA: Sage.

Hunter, G. (1996, May 29). Cost of hiring disabled minimized. *Louisville (KY) Courier-Journal,* p. A4.

Husserl, E. (1962). *Ideas: General introduction to pure phenomenology* (W. Gibson, Trans.). New York: Collier Books.

Husserl, E. (1964). *The idea of phenomenology.* The Hague: Marinus Nijhoff.

Hyde, M. J., & Smith, C. R. (1979). Hermeneutics and rhetoric: A seen but unobserved relationship. *Quarterly Journal of Speech, 65,* 347-363.

Ihde, D. (1977). *Experimental phenomenology: An introduction.* New York: Capricorn Books.

James, N. (1994). When Miss America was always white. In A. Gonzalez, M. Houston, & V. Chen (Eds.), *Our voices: Essays in culture, ethnicity, and communication* (pp. 43-47). Los Angeles, CA: Roxbury.

Jankowski, K. (1991). On communicating with deaf people. In L. A. Samovar & R. E. Porter (Eds.), *Intercultural communication: A reader* (pp. 142-149). Belmont, CA: Wadsworth.

Johnson, F. L. (1989). Women's culture and communication: An analytical perspective. In C. Cont & C. Friendly (Eds.), *Beyond boundaries: Sex and gender diversity in communication* (pp. 301-316). Fairfax, VA: George Mason University Press.

Kelley, H. H. (1979). *Personal relationships: Their structures and processes.* Hillside, NJ: Lawrence Erlbaum.

Kochman, T. (1990). Force fields in black and white communication. In D. Carbaugh (Ed.), *Cultural communication and intercultural contact* (pp. 193-217). Hillsdale, NJ: Lawrence Erlbaum.

Kramarae, C. (1978). Male and female perception of male and female speech. *Language and Speech, 20,* 151-161.

Kramarae, C. (1981). *Women and men speaking.* Rowley, MA: Newbury House.

Kreps, G. (1991, May). *Using the critical incident technique in health communication research: A narrative approach.* Paper presented at the annual meeting of the International Communication Association, Chicago, IL.

Krippendorff, K. (1989). The ethics of constructing communication. In B. Dervin, L. Grossberg, B. O'Keefe, & E. Wartella (Eds.), *Rethinking communication: Vol. 1. Paradigm issues* (pp. 78-87). Newbury Park, CA: Sage.

Lakoff, R. T. (1995). Cries and whispers: The shattering of silence. In K. Hall & M. Bucholtz (Eds.), *Gender articulated: Language and the socially constructed self* (pp. 25-50). Boston: Routledge Kegan Paul.

Langellier, K. M., & Hall, D. L. (1989). Interviewing women: A phenomenological approach to feminist communication research. In K. Carter & C. Spitzack (Eds.), *Doing research on women's communication: Perspectives on theory and method* (pp. 193-220). Norwood, NJ: Ablex.

Lanigan, R. L. (1979). The phenomenology of human communication. *Philosophy Today, 23*(i), 3-15.

Lanigan, R. L. (1988). *Phenomenology of communication: Merleau-Ponty's thematics in communicology and semiology.* Pittsburgh, PA: Duquesne University Press.

Le Guin, U. K. (1989). *Dancing at the edge of the world: Thoughts on words, women, places.* New York: Grove.

Lengel, L. (1992, October). *Investigating the gender differentiation of graduate student experience.* Paper presented at the annual meeting of the Midwest Popular Culture Association and the Midwest American Culture Association, Indianapolis, IN.

Leslie, K. B. (1997, April). *"Spread the word": Descriptions of ingroup/outgroup communication of transplant recipients.* Paper presented at the annual meeting of the Central States Communication Association, St. Louis, MO.

Lipman-Blumen, J. (1988, August). Connective leadership: A female perspective for an interdependent world. Invited address, Division 35, at the annual meeting of the American Psychological Association, Atlanta, GA.

Loden, M., & Rosener, J. B. (1991). *Workforce American! Managing employee diversity as a vital resource.* Homewood, IL: Business One Irwin.

Lorde, A. (1984). *Sister outsider.* Freedom, CA: Crossing Press.

Lovdal, L. (1989). *Speaking "like a woman" in Apple-Landia: Situated accomplishment of women who manage family, career, and children.* Unpublished doctoral dissertation, Ohio University, Athens.

Luna, A. (1989). Gay racism. In M. S. Kimmel & M. A. Messner (Eds.), *Men's lives* (pp. 440-448). New York: Macmillan.

Madison, D. S. (1993). "That was my occupation": Oral narrative, performance, and black feminist thought. *Text and Performance Quarterly, 13*(3), 213-232.

Marcel, G. (1950). *Mystery of being.* South Bend, IN: Gateway Editions.

McClenney, E. H. (1987). *How to survive when you're the only black in the office.* Richmond, VA: First Associates.

McIntosh, P. (1988). White privilege and male privilege: A personal account of coming to see correspondences through work in women's studies. *Wellesley College Center for Research on Women Working Paper Series, 189*, 1-19.

Meade, K. L. (1996, May). *Rethinking appropriateness: A look at hegemonic ideals as related to perceived communication competence in women*. Paper presented at the annual meeting of the International Communication Association, Chicago, IL.

Merleau-Ponty, M. (1962). *The visible and the invisible* (C. Smith, Trans., F. Williams, Trans. rev.). Boston: Routledge Kegan Paul. (Original work published in 1948)

Merleau-Ponty, M. (1964). *Signs*. Evanston, IL: Northwestern University Press.

Merleau-Ponty, M. (1968). *The prose of the world* (C. Ledford, Ed., A. Lingis, Trans.). Evanston, IL: Northwestern University Press.

Minister, K. (1991). A feminist frame for the oral history interview. In S. B. Gluck & D. Patai (Eds.), *Women's words: The feminist practice of oral history* (pp. 27-42). Boston: Routledge Kegan Paul.

Moon, D. G. (1996). Concepts of "culture": Implications for intercultural communication research. *Communication Quarterly, 44*(1), 70-84.

Nakayama, T. (1994). Dis/orienting identities: Asian Americans, history, and intercultural communication. In A. Gonzalez, M. Houston, & V. Chen (Eds.), *Our voices: Essays in culture, ethnicity, and communication* (pp. 133-139). Los Angeles, CA: Roxbury.

Nakayama, T. (1995). Disciplining evidence. *Western Journal of Communication, 59*, 171-175.

Nelson, J. (1986). *The other side of signification: A semiotic phenomenology of televisual experience*. Unpublished doctoral dissertation, Southern Illinois University at Carbondale.

Nelson, J. (1989a). Eyes out of your head: On televisual experience. *Critical Studies in Mass Communication, 6*, 387-403.

Nelson, J. (1989b). Phenomenology as feminist methodology: Explicating interviews. In K. Carter & C. Spitzack (Eds.), *Doing research on women's communication: Perspectives on theory and method* (pp. 221-241). Norwood, NJ: Ablex.

Nielsen, J. M. (Ed.). (1990). *Feminist research methods: Exemplary readings in the social sciences*. Boulder, CO: Westview.

O'Donnell, P. (1994, March 14). Look who's no longer missing the links. *Newsweek*, p. 68.

O'Leary, V. E. (1988). Women's relationships with women in the workplace. In B. A. Gutek, L. Larwood, & A. Stromberg (Eds.), *Women and work: An annual review* (Vol. 3, pp. 189-214). Newbury Park, CA: Sage.

O'Leary, V. E., & Ickovics, J. R. (1990). Women supporting women: Secretaries and their bosses. In H. Y. Grossman & N. L. Chester (Eds.), *The experience and meaning of work in women's lives* (pp. 35-56). Hillsdale, NJ: Lawrence Erlbaum.

Orbe, M. (1993). *"Remember, it's always whites' ball": A phenomenological inquiry into the African American male experience*. Unpublished doctoral dissertation, Ohio University, Athens.

Orbe, M. (1994a). Intercultural and co-cultural communication. In J. C. Pearson & P. E. Nelson's (Eds.), *Understanding and sharing: An introduction to speech communication* (pp. 186-206). Dubuque, IA: William C. Brown.

Orbe, M. (1994b). "Remember, it's always whites' ball": Descriptions of African American male communication. *Communication Quarterly, 42*(3), 287-300.

Orbe, M. (1995). African American communication research: Toward a deeper understanding of interethnic communication. *Western Journal of Communication, 59*(1), 61-78.

Orbe, M. (in press). Laying the foundation for co-cultural communication theory: An inductive approach to studying "non-dominant" communication strategies and the factors that influence them. *Communication Studies.*

Orbe, M., & Strother, K. E. (1996). Signifying the tragic mulatto: A semiotic analysis of "Alex Haley's Queen." *Howard Journal of Communication, 7*(2), 113-126.

Orbe, M., & Wilcoxson, K. (1995, November). *Is all interpersonal communication more aptly described as intercultural communication? Exploring how a communication axiom emerged from the unification of research, teaching, and service.* Paper presented at the annual meeting of the Speech Communication Association, San Antonio, TX.

Parrillo, V. N. (1996). *Diversity in America.* Thousand Oaks, CA: Pine Forge.

Patton, M. Q. (1983). *Qualitative evaluation methods.* London: Sage Ltd.

Pearson, J. C., & Nelson, P. E. (1991). *Understanding & sharing: An introduction to speech communication.* Dubuque, IA: William. C. Brown.

Pennington, D. L. (1979). Black-white communication: An assessment of research. In M. K. Asante, E. Newmark, & C. A. Blake (Eds.), *Handbook of intercultural communication* (pp. 383-402). Beverly Hills, CA: Sage.

Peterson, E. A. (1992). *African American woman: A study of will and success.* Jefferson, NC: McFarland.

Peterson, E. E. (1987). Media consumption and girls who want to have fun. *Critical Studies in Mass Communication, 4,* 37-50.

Philipsen, G. (1975). Speaking "like a man" in teamsterville: Culture patterns of role enactment in an urban neighborhood. *Quarterly Journal of Speech, 61,* 13-22.

Polkinghorne, D. (1983). *Methodology for the human sciences.* Albany: State University of New York Press.

Ravitch, D. (1990). Multiculturalism: E pluribus plures. *American Scholar, 59,* 337-354.

Ray, E. B., & Miller, K. I. (1991). The influence of communication structure and social support on job stress and burnout. *Management Communication Quarterly, 4,* 506-527.

Ribeau, S. A., Baldwin, J. R., & Hecht, M. L. (1994). An African-American communication perspective. In L. A. Samovar & R. E. Porter (Eds.), *Intercultural communication: A reader* (pp. 140-147). Belmont, CA: Wadsworth.

Ringer, R. J. (1994). *Queer words, queer images: Communication and the construction of homosexuality.* New York: New York University Press.

Roberts, G., & Orbe, M. (1996, May). *"Creating that safe place among family": Exploring intergenerational gay male communication.* Paper presented at the annual meeting of the International Communication Association, Chicago, IL.

Rose, H. (1983). Hand, brain, heart: A feminist epistemology for the natural sciences. *Signs, 9,* 73-90.

Samovar, L. A., & Porter, R. E. (1994). *Intercultural communication: A reader.* Belmont, CA: Wadsworth.

Sitaram, K. S., & Cogdell, R. T. (1976). *Foundations of intercultural communication.* Columbus, OH: Merrill.

Skinner, E. (1982). The dialectic between diaspora and homelands. In J. E. Harris (Ed.), *Global dimensions of the African diaspora* (pp. 17-45). Washington, DC: Howard University Press.
Slade, M. (1984, October 15). Relationships: Women and their secretaries. *New York Times*, p. 15.
Smith, D. E. (1987). *The everyday world as problematic: A feminist sociology of knowledge*. Boston: Northeastern University Press.
Smith, D. E. (1992). Sociology from women's experiences: A reaffirmation. *Sociological Theory, 10*(1), 1-12.
Snyder, M. (1974). The self-monitoring of expressive behavior. *Journal of Personality and Social Psychology, 30*, 526-537.
Spiegelberg, H. (1982). *The phenomenological movement* (3rd ed.). The Hague: Marinus Nijhoff. (Original work published 1960)
Spradlin, A. L. (1995, November). *The price of "passing": A lesbian perspective on authenticity in organizations*. Paper presented at the annual meeting of the Speech Communication Association, San Antonio, TX.
Stanage, S. (1987). *Adult education and phenomenological research*. Malabar, FL: Kreiger.
Stanback, M. H., & Pearce, W. B. (1981). Talking to "the man": Some communication strategies used by members of "subordinate" social groups. *Quarterly Journal of Speech, 67*, 21-30.
Steele, S. (1990). *The content of our character*. New York: St. Martin's.
Stockard, J., & Johnson, M. M. (1980). *Sex roles: Sex inequality and sex role development*. Englewood Cliffs, NJ: Prentice Hall.
Sutton, S. D., & Moore, K. K. (1985). Probing options: Executive women—20 years later. *Harvard Business Review, 85*(5), 42-66.
Swigonski, M. E. (1994). The logic of feminist standpoint theory for social work research. *Social Work, 39*(4), 387-393.
Thibaut, J. W., & Kelley, H. H. (1959). *The social psychology of groups*. New York: John Wiley.
Van Manen, M. (1990). *Researching lived experience: Human science for action sensitive pedagogy*. Ontario, Canada: State University of New York Press.
Wade, S. (1996, April 13). Consultant says conformity is a part of getting to the top. *Louisville (KY) Courier-Journal*, p. B14.
Wallace, R. A., & Wolf, A. (1995). *Contemporary sociological theory: Continuing the classical tradition*. Englewood Cliffs, NJ: Prentice Hall.
Warnick, B. (1979). Structuralism vs. phenomenology: Implications for rhetorical criticism. *Quarterly Journal of Speech, 65*, 250-261.
Wilson, G. L., Hantz, A. M., & Hanna, M. S. (1995). *Interpersonal growth through communication*. Dubuque, IA: William C. Brown.
Wilson, S. R., & Putnam, L. L. (1990). Interaction goals in negotiation. In J. A. Anderson (Ed.), *Communication yearbook 13* (pp. 374-406). Newbury Park, CA: Sage.
Wood, J. T. (1992). Gender and moral voice: Moving from woman's nature to standpoint epistemology. *Women's Studies in Communication, 15*(1), 1-24.
Woods, J. D. (1993). *The corporate closet: The professional lives of gay men in America*. New York: Free Press.

Index

About the Author

MARK P. ORBE received his Ph.D. in Interpersonal/Intercultural Communication from Ohio University in 1993. A faculty member in the Department of Communication at Western Michigan University, Orbe teaches and conducts research in the areas of interpersonal and intercultural communication, with a specific focus on cultural diversity in the United States. In the past 6 years, he has published more than 15 articles in communication-related journals and in edited books and presented close to 50 conference papers at regional, national, and international academic conventions. *Constructing Co-cultural Theory* is his first book-length manuscript.

Printed in the United States
130525LV00006B/205-213/A

9 780761 910688